# Harold Garfinkel

# Harold Garfinkel

The Creation and Development of Ethnomethodology

**Dirk vom Lehn**

**Left Coast Press Inc.**

Walnut Creek, California

Left Coast Press, Inc. is committed to preserving ancient
forests and natural resources. We elected to print this title on
30% post consumer recycled paper, processed chlorine free. As
a result, for this printing, we have saved:

2 Trees (40' tall and 6-8" diameter)
1 Million BTUs of Total Energy
146 Pounds of Greenhouse Gases
788 Gallons of Wastewater
53 Pounds of Solid Waste

Left Coast Press, Inc. made this paper choice because our
printer, Thomson-Shore, Inc., is a member of Green Press
Initiative, a nonprofit program dedicated to supporting
authors, publishers, and suppliers in their efforts to reduce
their use of fiber obtained from endangered forests.

For more information, visit www.greenpressinitiative.org

Environmental impact estimates were made using the Environmental Defense
Paper Calculator. For more information visit: www.papercalculator.org.

LEFT COAST PRESS, INC.
1630 North Main Street, #400
Walnut Creek, CA 94596
http://www.LCoastPress.com

ISBN 978-1-61132-979-7 hardcover
ISBN 978-1-61132-980-3 paperback
ISBN 978-1-61132-981-0 institutional eBook
ISBN 978-1-61132-754-0 consumer eBook

Library of Congress Cataloging-in-Publication Data:
Vom Lehn, Dirk.
    [Harold Garfinkel. English]
    Harold Garfinkel : the creation and development of ethnomethodology / Dirk
vom Lehn.
        pages   cm
    "A translated and updated version of Harold Garfinkel by Dirk vom Lehn,
published in 2013 in German by UVK Verlagsgesellschaft mbH.»
    Includes bibliographical references and index.
    ISBN 978-1-61132-979-7 (hardback : alk. paper)— ISBN 978-1-61132-980-3
(pbk. : alk. paper) — ISBN 978-1-61132-981-0 (institutional ebook) — ISBN
978-1-61132-754-0 (consumer ebook)
    1. Garfinkel, Harold.   2. Ethnomethodology.   3. Sociology.   I. Title.
HM481.V6613 2014
301—dc23
                                2013049057

Printed in the United States of America

∞^TM  The paper used in this publication meets the minimum requirements of American
National Standard for Information Sciences—Permanence of Paper for Printed Library
Materials, ANSI/NISO Z39.48-1992.

# Contents

# Foreword

*Studies in Ethnomethodology* was on my undergraduate reading list at the back end of the 1960s—but I am afraid that I parked it in favor of more fashionable work. I only really explored Garfinkel's work as a graduate student in Aberdeen in the early 1970s. I had the good fortune to encounter a brilliant group of mentors who were trying to piece it together with other strands from symbolic interactionism, dramaturgical sociology and social phenomenology. Different people took different positions within this project but it could be summed up as a search for an empirical study of social order founded in the detailed observation of what people said and did. Unlike much sociology of that period, they did not presume to know better than the participants what was really going on in any situation. Class, race and gender were not phenomena to be illustrated by selective quotation, but to be demonstrated as arising in and from interaction between people. Their relevance in any given situation was to be found rather than assumed. This did not prevent analysts having a range of personal sympathies or political convictions, but it was to assert, in the spirit of Weber's essays on science and politics as vocations, that a science of society was different from a normative analysis of society: the study of social order could be distinguished from the critique of a particular social order.

Garfinkel's writings were particularly important in developing this approach. Symbolic interactionism had struggled to escape from its pragmatist heritage and its associations with the reformist agenda of early Chicago sociology. Garfinkel cut through this with a clear and uncompromising reassertion of the core mission of sociology, fully in the tradition of Durkheim and, before him, Comte, to understand the accomplishment of orderliness in society. This did not prevent us from making moral judgments about the results—as his own early responses to racism showed—but it did insist that these had a different foundation and a different logic of argument. There was a meaningful life's work for a scientist of society in simply investigating the problem of order. Subsequently, it has also become clear that Garfinkel's work has a major role to play in exposing the nonsense that comes out of much popular neuroscience and evolutionary psychology. In one of his memorable aphorisms, Garfinkel observed that, if you wanted to know what went on in people's heads, you should become a brain surgeon. Unlike other micro-sociologies, ethnomethodology does not require a theory of mind. It deals only with what is observable and reportable—to ordinary people as much as to sociologists. Order is constructed from interactions between people—and possibly between people and objects—in ways that cannot be reduced to biological drives or cognitive processes.

As with any other radical innovator, Garfinkel faced the challenge of finding a new language in which to express his ideas. Just as it took a generation for most physicists to read Einstein correctly, so it has taken many years for the rest of us to grasp the details of his message. I once asked him whether English was his first language: Harold characteristically was more interested in why I had asked the question, but admitted that his family mostly spoke Yiddish and that he had not really been fluent in English until his early teens. As with many people who are self-taught, a fascination with the richness of language pervades his writing. Some passages are poetic in their intensity as they search for the vocabulary to give precise expression to his thoughts. This has been an important barrier for new students encountering his work. Dirk vom Lehn has performed a vital service to the whole sociological community by producing this book to help its readers make that transition. The whole body of Garfinkel's writing is explored—from early career writings that have only been published in recent years, to the re-energized intellectual radicalism of his late works, where he located ethnomethodology's concern for orderliness as an authentic tradition in sociology. This book explains key elements of Garfinkel's thinking in more accessible language and smooths the way to reading the originals.

Garfinkel had many struggles for respect and recognition in his lifetime. His legacy, however, is one for the ages—to challenge, provoke and inspire sociologists of all generations, backgrounds and persuasions to think harder about what they are trying to achieve and how to achieve it. As the Chinese philosopher, Laozi, noted, the longest journey begins from where you stand now. Dirk has created your guidebook (or sat nav if you are reading an e-book!).

*Robert Dingwall*
*Dingwall Enterprises*
*Nottingham, United Kingdom*
*June 2013*

# Acknowledgments

I was first introduced to ethnomethodology and conversation analysis by the late Anne Honer. Anne was an extraordinary scholar and teacher who, in her seminars, confounded us with data from her research. These data included field notes, audio-recordings, field observations, and transcripts that we analyzed in light of reading papers by Schutz and Luckmann as well as the famous "Systematics" paper by Sacks, Schegloff, and Jefferson (1974). My interest in ethnomethodology and conversation analysis developed further when, as a doctoral student, I moved to Nottingham, where I joined Christian Heath, Jon Hindmarsh, and Paul Luff at the Work, Interaction, and Technology Research Group. Over the past seventeen years, first at the University of Nottingham and then at King's College London, I have been extraordinarily lucky to work with this team of colleagues and friends who have been incredibly supportive. Their influence on the content of this book will be noted by those familiar with their work. I cannot thank them enough for introducing me to the practice of conducting ethnomethodological research and video-based studies of interaction.

The quality of the book was immensely improved by a number of very kind colleagues and friends to whom I owe for their time and effort in reading and commenting on an earlier draft of this manuscript. Neil Jenkings, Anne Rawls, Philippe Sormani, Roy Turner and Patrick Watson provided me with valuable information on Garfinkel's life and work. Thank you!

A related "thank you" goes to Helena Webb and Andrea Coleman who helped with the editing of the book and improved an originally very rough draft. Errors, mistakes, and misunderstandings that have remained in the final version of the manuscript are, of course, nobody else's but my own shortcomings.

The book is based on an original German version that I published in 2012 with UVK Verlagsgesellschaft in Konstanz. Robert Dingwall encouraged me to translate that manuscript and helped me find a suitable publisher for the English version that uses parts of the original German version. He also was incredibly kind in writing a very supportive foreword to this book that captures very well also my motivation for writing the book.

At UVK Verlagsgesellschaft I would like to thank Ines Ende and Sonja Rothländer who helped with the transfer of rights to Left Coast Press. The excellent staff at Left Coast Press, Inc. remained very patient despite my late submission of the final manuscript to them. Very many thanks to Mitch Allen who invited me to write the book and nudged me onward when I was late and then very late in submitting it, to Kathleen Rake (Click Media Works) for her help in preparing the manuscript for publication, Kirsten Kite for her meticulous proofreading, to Detta Penna for turning the manuscript into a book, and to Christine Longmuir (Left Coast Press) for helping with the publication process.

# Introduction

Harold Garfinkel is the founder of *ethnomethodology*. His ground-breaking *Studies in Ethnomethodology* published in 1967 has fundamentally challenged sociology as a discipline. In the 1970s, some saw the book as a major threat to sociology, others wrote it off as irrelevant to the discipline. *Studies* implies a radical shift in sociological perspective, without abandoning sociology. In fact, Garfinkel's more recent books, *Ethnomethodology's Program* (2002) and *Seeing Sociologically* (2006 [1948]) emphasize that, as a sociologist, his thinking was always grounded in the works of Durkheim and Parsons. Although some sociologists consider ethnomethodology as rather marginal, *Studies* is one of the most influential contributions to sociology, and ethnomethodology features in most recent textbooks of the discipline (Appelrouth and Edles 2007; Denzin and Lincoln 2011; Fulcher and Scott 2007; Giddens 2009). Moreover, the *sociological attitude* that Garfinkel began to develop and elaborate on from the 1940s and the insights his ethnomethodological program of studies has produced have been incorporated into the sociological mainstream, often without awareness of their origin in Garfinkel's original writings.

This book is not an introduction to ethnomethodology. Instead, my principal aim is to explicate the development of ethnomethodology from Garfinkel's early writings in the 1930s and 1940s, and to demonstrate ethnomethodology's grounding in and contribution to sociology. Thus, with this small book I also hope to reinvigorate reflection on ethnomethodology's contribution to sociology within what some might call mainstream sociology. What follows adds to this reflection and explains Garfinkel's and ethnomethodology's place within and contribution to sociology, by tracing the development of the key principles of what now is known as *Ethnomethodology's Program* (Garfinkel 1996, 2002).

The book has been written for students of sociology and cognate disciplines who have an interest in ethnomethodology and would like to discover more about the origin and motivation that drove Garfinkel to develop this particular *sociological attitude* to studying and describing the practices that continuously assemble the social world. It updates and complements, but does not replace, those fabulous books on ethnomethodology and conversation analysis by Kenneth Leiter (1980), John Heritage (1984), Douglas Benson and John Hughes (1983), Richard Hilbert (1992), Paul ten Have (2004) and, most recently, Kenneth Liberman's (2013) *More Studies in Ethnomethodology*. These and many other books on ethnomethodology have been written by well-known scholars who have long undertaken ethnomethodological research and are books that have served and will continue to serve as introductions to ethnomethodology for students and academics in the future.

This book focuses on the development of ethnomethodology by Harold Garfinkel since the 1940s. It begins with a brief introduction to Garfinkel's journey, from his father's furniture business in Newark (New Jersey) to Talcott Parsons' Department of Social Relations in Harvard. I take this journey as the starting-point to trace Garfinkel's (1991) *respecification* of what he sometimes called "traditional sociology" itself. In doing so, I explore, in particular, how Garfinkel used the different theoretical foundations underlying Talcott Parsons' theory of social order and Alfred Schutz's social phenomenology to develop his own *sociological attitude* (Garfinkel 2006 [1948]). In light of this theoretical exploration, I then investigate how Garfinkel advanced concepts of *account* and *accounting* that later became key to practicing ethnomethodology (and conversation analysis). This discussion of Garfinkel's creation of a *sociological attitude* provides the basis for the further development of ethnomethodology and Garfinkel's interest in the (practical) orderliness of the everyday, something central to his theoretical, methodological, and empirical program.

His concept of *order* or *social organization*, as demonstrated in later parts of this book, offers a fundamentally novel way to address sociology's most fundamental question: "How is social order possible?" This question dates back to debates in social philosophy and sociology by the ancient Greeks and by Hobbes in the 17th century, as well as to the important theoretical contributions of Garfinkel's dissertation advisor, Talcott Parsons. These social thinkers primarily answered the question of social order by referring to the existence of an external framework, such as a "Leviathan" (Hobbes), a "social contract" (Rousseau), or a shared set of values acquired through education and socialization (Parsons). Garfinkel, however, argued against *an order from without* and for *an order from within*; in other words, he was interested in how people in concrete situations produce their actions in ways that they and others recognize and understand to be "orderly" and intelligibly organized.

This book introduces these ideas which Garfinkel had already discussed in his early, but unpublished, writings. It also elaborates on how he then further developed these ideas in discussion with Talcott Parsons at Harvard, Alfred Schutz, and Aron Gurwitsch, with whom he regularly met for evening seminars in New York (Psathas 2004). By briefly exploring Garfinkel's intellectual relationship with Parsons and Schutz I discuss the emergence of ethnomethodology and some of its key principles explicated by Garfinkel in various publications since the 1970s. The purpose of this part of the book is to explore the origins of some of these principles and consider how they provide the basis for the development of various strands of ethnomethodological research. These strands include: conversation analysis and studies of institutional talk; social studies of science; and workplace studies. The final chapters investigate ethnomethodology's relationship to sociology, and how a number of research areas in the social sciences and elsewhere have been influenced by Garfinkel's writings to the present day, even though some of his studies are more than fifty years old.

# Chapter 1

# Sociology as a "Love Affair"

Harold Garfinkel was born on October 29, 1917 in Newark, New Jersey. The early 1920s were dominated by the First World War, ethnic tensions, and economic uncertainty. His father, Abraham Garfinkel, was a furniture trader in the large Jewish community of Newark, which, at that time, was characterized by a large number of immigrants who were concerned about their social and economic well-being. Like the rest of the USA, the world economic crisis of the 1920s hit this community badly and increased social and economic uncertainty among people. These developments also affected Garfinkel's upbringing and life-experience as a young person. From an early age onward, Garfinkel experienced what it meant to live in a marginal community with people, "who were struggling not only to find a place in American society but to formulate that place in their own terms" (Rawls 2002: 9). An interest in social issues therefore came naturally to him.

When in 1935, at the age of seventeen, Garfinkel proposed that he would like to study at university, his father was concerned that his son should learn a trade that could earn him a living (Rawls 2003a: 18). When the matter of the young Garfinkel's career was discussed in the family, a non-Jewish in-law, who was seen as knowledgeable regarding job prospects outside the Newark Jewish community, was asked for advice. He spoke with Garfinkel Junior, who, at the time had an interest in becoming a surgeon, a profession that, in the view of the in-law, was like "driving taxicabs"; it was the Depression (Rawls 2003a: 11). A compromise was found and Garfinkel agreed to work in his father's business in the evenings, while during the day he attended an unaccredited program at the University of Newark (today known as the Newark Campus of Rutgers University), majoring in business and accounting. Here, Garfinkel was introduced to the "theory of accounting" and double-entry bookkeeping. He learned that the placing of items in the columns of accounts not only constructs accounts, but also is a practice that is accountable to superiors and other agencies (Rawls 2002: 10). Later, Garfinkel considered his studies of accounting and bookkeeping as being more important for his later work on accounts than his studies of C. Wright Mills and Kenneth Burke's social theories of accounts (ibid.).

As suggested by Rawls (2003a: 19), there are quite obvious connections between the approach to accounting that Garfinkel was taught at the University of Newark and his later work. As Garfinkel developed as a sociologist, he related the accounting knowledge he had acquired at Newark and in his father's business to the analysis of everyday interaction. Just as the accountant is *accountable* for his work, the everyday actor is *accountable* for her/his action. Everyday actions are *accounts* and *accountable* just like the inputting of data by accountants; they are "observable-and-reportable" (Garfinkel 1967c: 1) actions that actors are accountable for, because they are visible as the producers of the action.[1] In later chapters, I return to Garfinkel's concepts of *account* and *accounting* as practical action and their implications for Garfinkel's sociology.

At the University of Newark, Garfinkel developed friendships with students and tutors who became important for his later career (Rawls 2002: 11). They included Melvin Tumin (later an anthropologist at Princeton), Herbert McClosky (later a political scientist at Berkeley), and Seymour Sarason (later a psychiatrist at Yale University). He also made the acquaintance of Philip Selznick (later a sociologist at UCLA) and Paul Lazarsfeld, who taught a course on social statistics at the University of Newark and, since the 1940s, has become famous for the foundation of what today would be called *scientific sociology* and empirical research methods. In discussion with his fellow students and friends, Garfinkel developed an interest in sociology and philosophy (Rawls 2002: 11).

After graduating from the University of Newark in 1939, Garfinkel attended a Quaker work camp in Georgia, and used the time to decide about his future. He discussed possibilities with Morris Mitchell, from the Columbia School of Education, who recommended the sociology department at the University of North Carolina in Chapel Hill to him. In Chapel Hill, Howard Odum had founded the Department of Sociology in 1920 and the Institute for Research in Social Science in 1924 (Brazil 1988). I return to Garfinkel's studies at Odum's Institute in North Carolina and to his master's thesis in 1942, his first formal sociological study, in later chapters.

In the summer of 1939, Garfinkel purchased Talcott Parsons' classic two-volume book *The Structure of Social Action* (1937). His reading of this book immediately drew him to sociology, and he became involved in sociological debates and thinking: "According to Garfinkel it was a 'love affair' from the beginning" (Rawls 2002: 13). At the time, sociology was a discipline that included a range of theories and methods. Odum's teaching in Chapel Hill highlighted the social action theory of Florian Znaniecki and William I. Thomas, as well as the pragmatist theories of action and interaction developed by Charles Horton Cooley and George Herbert Mead.

Garfinkel pursued his studies in sociology and developed an interest in studies of social justice and the social organization of everyday life. This emerging interest in sociology is reflected in his prizewinning short story entitled "Color Trouble" (Garfinkel 1940) that he wrote in the late 1930s. The story describes how passengers on a public bus negotiate the public order defined by racial segregation with the bus driver and police. As the passengers, driver, and police officers discuss and challenge the reasoning for the public order, they make intelligible the foundation of the social order on the bus.

At this point, Garfinkel had not yet developed a sociological vocabulary to explain the events on the bus. He did not yet talk of a "pluralism of worlds" (Garfinkel 1952: 97) or of "accounts" (Garfinkel 1967a) that later defined some of his studies (Doubt 1989; Rawls 2013). I return to the events Garfinkel described in this short story and their relevance to his sociology in more detail in the next chapter, "Hitchhiking to Sociology."

Following the completion of his MA thesis at North Carolina in 1942, Garfinkel joined the US Air Force and undertook a field study concerning "the effects of temporary military industry on the social organization of the town of Bastrop Texas" (Rawls 2008b: 6) for the sociologist Wilbert Moore (1914–1987), whom he met again later in his career, in the early 1950s. Having joined the US Air Force, Garfinkel was given the task of training soldiers on a golf course on Miami Beach in preparation for tank combat in Europe (Rawls 2002: 14–15).

In 1946, after the war, Garfinkel moved to Harvard and began his studies for a PhD with Talcott Parsons and in 1952 completed his dissertation, *The Perception of the Other: A Study in Social Order* (Rawls 2002: 15). In this dissertation he critically assessed Parsons' social theory by drawing on Alfred Schutz's (1967b [1932]) phenomenological analysis. While undertaking his studies, Garfinkel regularly met with Schutz and also with Aron Gurwitsch in New York to discuss phenomenological questions and their relevance to sociology (Barber 2004; Psathas 2004; Rawls 2002). The influence of these discussions on Garfinkel's sociological thinking is clearly visible throughout his work. He used Schutz and Gurwitsch's phenomenological analyses to develop a novel approach to explore social order. His approach was not determined by phenomenology, but he creatively used the phenomenological focus on the actor's point of view to create a *sociological attitude* to analyze the social world that later he called *ethnomethodology*.

The development of Garfinkel's sociological attitude became apparent in a manuscript that Anne Rawls recently published under the title, *Seeing Sociologically* (Garfinkel 2006 [1948]). In this book, Garfinkel argued for the need to adopt this particular sociological attitude to enable the analysis of how actors in the *natural attitude* produce and experience social order (Garfinkel 2006 [1948]: 127–129). Here, he drew on Alfred Schutz (1945b),who had developed the concept of *natural attitude* to understand how an actor in ordinary circumstances acts in and upon, and experiences the everyday world. In later chapters, in particular when discussing *Seeing Sociologically* and Garfinkel's PhD dissertation, I examine how Schutz's concept of natural attitude provided Garfinkel with the basis for the development of the sociological attitude that underpins ethnomethodology. I explore how Garfinkel used Schutz's interpretation of phenomenology in his PhD dissertation to develop an independent sociological perspective that differed from that of his doctoral advisor, Talcott Parsons.

While Garfinkel studied for his PhD, he taught for two years at Princeton University (New Jersey) and, in 1952, together with Richard Snyder and Wilbert Moore, organized a conference entitled, "Problems in Model Construction in the Social Sciences" (Rawls 2003a: 23). The theme of the conference arose from the context of a project funded by the Ford Foundation and it was attended by major social scientists of the time, including Talcott Parsons, Paul Lazarsfeld, Herbert Simon, Kenneth Burke, Alfred Schutz, and Kurt Wolff. During his time at Princeton, Garfinkel also worked on various manuscripts, some of which were recently published by Anne Rawls under the title, *Toward a Sociological Theory of Information* (Garfinkel 2008).

Meeting Kurt Wolff at the Princeton conference may well have helped Garfinkel a few years later to find a job at the University of Ohio, where Wolff was directing a research project concerned with leadership in organizations. Having received his PhD from Harvard, Garfinkel joined Wolff in Ohio for a two-year position (Rawls 2003a: 23). However, when this project was curtailed due to budget cuts, his friend Fred Strodtbeck, a classmate from Harvard, asked Garfinkel to join him and Saul Mendlovitz at the University of Wichita (Kansas) to work on a research project that has become known as the "Jury Project" (Kalven 1966; Rawls 2003a: 23). As part of the project, Garfinkel studied the organization of jury deliberations in courts and analyzed audio-recordings of jury deliberations that Strodtbeck had produced as data for the project. In summer 1954, Garfinkel and his colleagues Strodtbeck and Mendlovitz presented parts of their research at the annual conference of the American Sociological Association (ASA). Here, they used for the first time the term *ethnomethods* to describe actions that become intelligible as "methods" used by a particular group ("ethnos"), i.e., jury members, because the group members produce the actions in ways jury members do for their practical purposes.

In 1954, following the ASA conference, Garfinkel was once again looking for work and a more permanent position. His subsequent move to UCLA, where he remained for the rest of his academic career, was supported by his friends Philip Selznick (1919–2010) and Melvin Tumin (1919–1994), whom he had first met while studying at Newark. By then Selznick had become an influential sociologist at UCLA and had moved to UC Berkeley in 1952, while Tumin developed his career at Princeton. They both persuaded the then chair of the Department of Sociology at UCLA to hire Garfinkel in 1954 as an Assistant Professor (Rawls 2003: 24).

One of the best known of Garfinkel's colleagues, Harvey Sacks (1935–1975), invented the study of conversation (Silverman 1998) and together with Gail Jefferson and Emanuel Schegloff further developed what now is known as *conversation analysis* (Sacks 1992; Schegloff 1989, 2007a). Sacks studied for a bachelor's degree at Columbia College and after its completion in 1955 was awarded a scholarship at Yale Law School, where in 1959 he earned an undergraduate law degree (LLB). As he studied the law, he became interested in "how the law as an institution worked" rather "than in making it work as an attorney himself" (Schegloff 1992: xii–xiii). With this intellectual interest, Sacks enrolled in Political Science at MIT and worked as a research assistant in the Department of Economics and Social Science. He attended seminars by Noam Chomsky at MIT and advanced his interests in how decisions are made in judicial processes and how to adequately describe these processes sociologically (Silverman 1998). Through this interest he was spurred to attend a seminar given by Talcott Parsons in Cambridge, where he met Garfinkel, who was spending a sabbatical at Harvard (1959) (Schegloff 1992: xiii).

Sacks and Garfinkel liked each other and developed an intellectual relationship that lasted until Sacks' premature death in 1975 (Schegloff 1992: xiii). They discussed questions of social order, judicial processes, and sociological descriptions that were at the heart of Garfinkel's current and early studies. Sacks did not see how he could effectively pursue these questions at MIT and decided to move to Berkeley and study sociology. He made this decision in light of his discussions with Garfinkel and on the advice of Harold Lasswell (1902–1978), a professor of law with expertise in political science and communications theory, whom he knew from his studies at Yale (Schegloff 1992: xiii).

In 1960, Sacks moved to Berkeley where he continued to pursue his interest in judicial processes and later became the first graduate fellow in the Center for the Study of Law and Society that Philip Selznick founded and chaired from 1961 to 1972. His PhD advisor, however, was not Selznick, but Erving Goffman, whose influence on Sacks' intellectual development is visible in publications such as "Notes on police assessment of moral character" (Sacks 1972) and in many of his lectures (Silverman 1998: 32–36). Nevertheless, Garfinkel remained a key influence on Sacks' academic work and he stayed in close contact with him throughout his doctoral project. He invited Garfinkel to Berkeley where he, as well as other ethnomethodologists like Egon Bittner (1921–2011) and Aaron Cicourel, talked at the Graduate Sociology Club. Sacks also attended conferences at UCLA organized by Garfinkel and his colleague Edward Rose of the University of Colorado and read and privately circulated Garfinkel's then still-unpublished manuscripts among graduate students in sociology (Schegloff 1992: xiv–xv).

Garfinkel's manuscripts provided Sacks and his colleagues at Berkeley with a wealth of material to discuss (Schegloff 1992). These colleagues included David Sudnow, who studied the organization of dying in a hospital and also became well known for his research on piano playing (Sudnow 1967, 1979); Roy Turner, who published the first collection of ethnomethodological articles (Turner 1974); Emanuel Schegloff, who later cooperated with Sacks and Gail Jefferson on the development of *conversational analysis*[2], and others. In 1963/64, Garfinkel encouraged Sacks to move to UCLA and take up a position as Acting Assistant Professor of Sociology (Schegloff 1992: xv). Here, they cooperated on a research project as Fellows at the Center for the Scientific Study of Suicide in Los Angeles, under the sponsorship of its director, Edwin Shneidman (Schegloff 1992: xv). As part of the project, Sacks examined short fragments of telephone conversations in great detail. This analysis of calls to the Suicide Prevention Center formed the basis of Sacks' doctoral research and can be regarded as the origin of conversation analysis (Sacks 1966; Schegloff 1992).

At the same time, Garfinkel worked on at least two book manuscripts that remain unpublished to the present day. The first of these is *Parsons' Primer*, an examination of Parsons' investigation of the problem of social order. The manuscript reflected Garfinkel's admiration for the work of his doctoral advisor and dismissed critiques of Parsons' theory as trivial and irrelevant. However, it also revealed that Garfinkel, now forty-three years old, was not entirely in agreement with Parsons. As Rawls (2013: 310) suggests, Garfinkel criticized Parsons for developing a theory of social action from the actor's point of view that loses both the interaction and the actor.

The second unpublished manuscript (1962) is a collection of articles entitled *Some Sociological Methods for Making Everyday Activities Observable*. It comprises eighteen chapters that discussed theoretical, methodological, and empirical questions (Schegloff 1999). Some of the chapters from this manuscript were later published in academic journals and in Garfinkel's *Studies in Ethnomethodology* (Garfinkel 1967a). A number of these chapters, as well as different versions of *Parsons' Primer*, circulate as gray, still unpublished literature among ethnomethodologists.[3]

In 1967 Garfinkel published *Studies in Ethnomethodology*, the book that ever since has defined ethnomethodology. While some of the chapters in this book had largely been ignored when they were published in academic journals, their publication in *Studies* stimulated vigorous, sometimes hostile debates at conferences and workshops (Coser 1975; Gellner 1975; Goldthorpe 1973), as well as a large number of book reviews in major journals (Coleman, Bruyn, and Wallace 1968; Busfield 1968; Swanson, Wallace, and Coleman 1968; Wilkins 1968). While some berated Garfinkel as a "charlatan" and leader of a sect (Coser 1975),[4] others considered ethnomethodology to be in intellectual opposition to Parsons' functionalism and the growth of quantitative empirical social research. This polarization of ethnomethodology and "traditional" or "conventional" sociology was reinforced by the sometimes polemical tone Garfinkel and his colleagues used in some of their publications (Garfinkel and Wieder 1992; Garfinkel and Sacks 1970). Up to the present day, textbooks of sociology consider ethnomethodology as an important strand within the discipline, but see Garfinkel and the ethnomethodologists as marginal and often characterize ethnomethodology inadequately, by arguing that Garfinkel ignores sociological theory. In later chapters of this book, I discuss the relationship of Garfinkel's ethnomethodology to "traditional" sociological theories and methods.

In the 1970s, Garfinkel spent sabbaticals in Manchester (1973), Stanford (1975/76), and Oxford (1979/80).[5] During his sabbaticals he further developed his approach to teaching and research in sociology and became interested in studying the work practices of scientists. Together with Michael Lynch and Eric Livingstone, Garfinkel established the ethnomethodological studies of science that reveal the social production of scientific discoveries (Garfinkel, Lynch, and Livingston 1981; Lynch, Garfinkel, and Livingston 1983). Drawing on his analysis of the work of scientists, Garfinkel also developed a further interest in the sociology of work and edited a book entitled *Ethnomethodological Studies of Work* (Garfinkel 1986). This volume included an article that he had previously published with Harvey Sacks (Garfinkel and Sacks 1970) and contributions by some of his students that were concerned with the "praxeology"[6] of "work" in settings and domains that were not conventionally considered work, such as Kung Fu training and the hermeneutics of the occult.

After retiring from his chair at UCLA in 1987, Garfinkel continued his elaboration of the ethnomethodological program whereby his analyses explored the relationship between "the perspective of ethnomethodology," as Benson and Hughes (1983) call it, and the sociologies developed by Durkheim and Parsons. Publications deriving from this work were designed to highlight that ethnomethodology is an "alternate" (not an alternative!) to traditional sociology. Traditional sociology relies on a specific interpretation of Durkheim with which Garfinkel did not agree.

This critique of traditional sociology pervades Garfinkel's publications. As time progressed, he increasingly highlighted his interpretation of Durkheim that, in his view, was closer to Durkheim's original writing than the interpretation generally disseminated in sociological textbooks. For example, in *Ethnomethodology's Program,* Garfinkel (1996, 2002) argued that it was not ethnomethodology, but sociology that had removed itself from Durkheim's program. He suggested that traditional sociological research had created a vast corpus of literature that now formed the basis for the "contemporary worldwide social science movement" (Garfinkel 2002: 65); however, it was not helpful in illuminating the phenomenon of *social order* that is at the heart of Durkheim's (and Parsons') work because, as Garfinkel argued, it instead generated theories and concepts that differed from people's experience of the life-world. To really understand social phenomena Garfinkel claimed that it was necessary to adopt a *sociological attitude.* In his view, this sociological attitude could not be acquired through conventional methods of teaching and training or the reading of academic literature, but it would require methods that allowed the student to experience the production of social order first hand. For this purpose Garfinkel (2002) developed tutorial exercises that made intelligible the fact that social order is inherent to the production of every action.

As emeritus professor at UCLA, Garfinkel's contribution to sociology was recognized by various international institutions. In 1995, he received the Cooley-Mead Award from the ASA Section Social Psychology for Distinguished Scholarship (Maynard 1996) in 1998 he was awarded an honorary doctorate from the University of Nottingham; and in 2007 he received the EMCA Lifetime Achievement Award of the ASA Section "Ethnomethodology and Conversation Analysis." He also participated in international workshops and conferences organized by Lucy Suchman at PARC (Xerox, Palo Alto), the ASA Section "Ethnomethodology and Conversation Analysis," and the "International Institute of Ethnomethodology and Conversation Analysis." Until his death on April 21, 2011, Garfinkel maintained his interest in exploring the social organization of the everyday. In doing so, he was concerned with diverse phenomena that center upon the embodied practices through which participants in concrete situations generate order.

Garfinkel's empirical research was based on very detailed observations of everyday phenomena. For his analysis of these phenomena he deployed a particular *sociological attitude* or a *cognitive style* that he developed from the 1940s onwards. In the following chapter, I begin to explore the development of this attitude by examining the emergence of his intellectual and academic interest in sociological questions and concerns.

# Chapter 2

# Hitch-hiking to Sociology

In 1939 Garfinkel decided to study sociology at Chapel Hill, North Carolina, after discussing his future with Morris Mitchell, who at the time worked at the Columbia School of Education. Mitchell's advice to Garfinkel was to move to the Department of Sociology, which had been established in 1920 by Howard Odum and where, since 1924, the Institute for Research in Social Science had conducted very influential research into social inequality and interethnic relationships (Brazil 1988; Johnson 1955; Rawls 2002). Following Mitchell's advice, Garfinkel decided to study in North Carolina and, from the Quaker summer camp in Georgia, hitch-hiked directly to Chapel Hill to become a sociologist (Rawls 2002).

On his arrival in Chapel Hill, Garfinkel went directly to Howard Odum's home and told him that while he was without financial means, he would like to study sociology with him. When talking about the event with Anne Rawls, Garfinkel recalled that in response to his question, Odum looked at him and said; "You are a New York Jew who has come to the country. I'll support you" (Garfinkel in Rawls 2002: 11). Garfinkel obtained a stipend and fulfilled his dream of studying sociology.

This chapter traces Garfinkel's development as a sociologist up to the submission and eventual publication of his master's thesis. The chapter begins with Garfinkel's experiences of ethnic segregation in North Carolina and his studies at Howard Odum's Institute for Research in Social Science. The discussion focuses on the short story (1940)[1] Garfinkel wrote and published in the late 1930s and on his master's thesis.

*Harold Garfinkel: The Creation and Development of*
*Ethnomethodology* by Dirk vom Lehn. 29–38. © 2013 UVK
Verlagsgesellschaft mbH; additional material for English
edition © 2014 Left Coast Press, Inc. All rights reserved.

## "Color Trouble"—A Short Story

In the 1930s and 1940s, life in North Carolina and parts of the southern states of the USA was characterized by ethnic segregation. On public transportation, African Americans were only permitted to travel in the backseats of public buses, and African American men were not allowed to smile at white women, and certainly not allowed to establish personal relationships with them. Garfinkel, who himself had grown up in an immigrant community, was sensitive to the problems that arose from such regulations for people in the everyday. Based on personal experiences, he wrote the short story "Color Trouble" in winter 1939, which depicted his observations on a bus journey from Washington, DC to Durham in North Carolina.[2]

At the heart of the story are various participants' diverging perspectives on the only seemingly objective, normative order. The story begins when the bus arrives on time in Petersburg (Virginia), one of the stops on the journey. At this stop, a young black woman boards the bus with a friend. The driver tells the pair, the two main actors in the story, to take two seats at the back of the bus. The pair object to the instruction and create a major argument that progressively escalates.

Because the driver is responsible for the timely arrival of the bus at each destination, in cases of delays he needs to explain or account for late departures and arrivals to his passengers and supervisors. One of the accounts drivers routinely gave for delays was "color trouble." The drivers referred to "color trouble" as an account when their journeys were delayed because non-white passengers resisted their instructions to conduct themselves in particular ways. Color trouble arose when drivers who asked African American passengers to sit at the back of the bus were challenged by these passengers and asked to give reasons for the request.

In Garfinkel's short story, the driver of the bus refers to the legislation in Virginia where the bus has stopped. The pair persistently reject the request of the driver, who then decides to call the police to help him restore order on the bus and make sure he can continue his journey in a timely fashion. On arrival of the police, the driver once again refers to the law to explain his request for the pair to move to the back of the bus. The pair refer to a different normative order, namely the American constitution that, in their view, assures all citizens the same rights including the right to freely choose where to sit on the bus. Moreover, they point out that the seats the driver had asked them to sit in were damaged. As the argument persists and time goes by, the other passengers become impatient and begin to complain about the delay to their journey. The events continue and eventually arrive at crisis point when the police decide to arrest the pair and take them away to the police station.

Events like those in Garfinkel's story were observed on a regular basis in the American south of the 1930s, as Johnson (1941), Garfinkel's master's thesis advisor said in an article, "Perhaps truth is *stronger* than fiction!" (Johnson 1941: 95–96, Fn3). And indeed, a few years later civil disobedience contributed a great deal to the Civil Rights Movement in the USA. In 1955, Rosa Parks refused to follow the instructions of a bus driver in Montgomery (Alabama), triggering events that led to a boycott of public transportation in Montgomery and a court hearing that eventually declared the unequal treatment of ethnic groups by bus companies in Alabama to be unconstitutional (Davis 1999).

Garfinkel wrote this story when he had just taken up his studies in sociology. However, its analytic orientation already pointed to his interest in the significance of *accounts* that actors produce in social situations to provide explanations for their actions and those of others, i.e., to explain the basis for the social order they experience and accomplish (cf. Rawls 2002: 14). It also makes clear that in the same situation, people might orient to and experience the social world in very different ways causing a "clash of perceptions" (Garfinkel 1952: 269) that requires the pair, the passengers, the drivers, and the police officers to give accounts that are designed to normalize the situation (cf. Hama 2009).

As the story unfolds, the reader sees how color trouble is used as an external institutional account to overwrite the reasonable request by the pair to be treated as equals among the other passengers (Rawls 2013). S/he then gets to observe how a particular social order, based on an institutionally legitimized account, is practically instantiated and exhibited: when passengers place their bodies in particular seats on the bus in response to requests and demands by the driver or the police; when the police physically remove the passengers from the bus to restore the social order they see instantiated in the state legislation; or when the other passengers refer to the official time-table when displaying impatience about the bus delay. We can therefore see that already in the early 1940s, Garfinkel showed his awareness for the power of institutional accountability as embodied in the explanations given by the driver and the police officers, and how this power can disrupt und undermine the trust relationships between actors in ordinary interaction. The driver can "enforce unjust rules about race without penalty to himself" (Rawls 2013: 308).

## The Social Order in Court

The content of the above story was related to the research that Howard Odum and his colleagues conducted at the Department of Sociology at the University of North Carolina. At the time, Odum was particularly interested in interracial relations. His colleague Guy B. Johnson, who advised Garfinkel on his studies, supported the young student's interest in sociology and introduced him to, among others, the sociology of William I. Thomas. Garfinkel also concerned himself with the works of Florian Znaniecki who had become famous for the book *The Polish Peasant in Europe and America* (1920), which he had jointly published with Thomas. Garfinkel particularly valued Znaniecki's book *Social Actions* (1936) and in reading it he became interested in developing a sociological perspective that allowed him to study the perspective actors themselves adopt in situations. He also read C. Wright Mills' (1940) article "Situated actions and vocabularies of motive" and Kenneth Burke's (1992 [1945]) examination of theories of the attribution of motives. These two authors, as well as Karl Mannheim, later became of particular importance for Garfinkel's development of *accounts* and of the *documentary method of interpretation* that I will discuss in the chapter "What is Ethnomethodology?"

Guy B. Johnson invited Garfinkel to join a team of researchers to work on one of his projects. The project was concerned with exploring whether it could be shown that Whites and African Americans were treated differently by the courts when accused of an offense. Johnson doubted that it was sufficient to explain this statistical observation by referring to social condemnation and economic discrimination against African Americans. He investigated economic and social reasons for the observation and argued that in the 1930s the African American population often lived in ghettos and in ostracized economic conditions. They were not permitted to participate fully in society and could be indicted for actions that were seen as inoffensive when conducted by white Americans. In one of his publications that already included Garfinkel's analysis, Johnson (1941) listed a number of incidents that were considered public nuisances or even offenses, such as violations of the segregation laws on buses and in other public areas. Together with his research team, Johnson analyzed public statistics of such incidents and drew the conclusion that the indictment and conviction of people was systematically related to the participants' ethnic backgrounds. Johnson believed that the statistics obfuscated the organized bias against African Americans in court, a bias that resulted from their marginalization in US society.

In a later publication, Johnson and Johnson (1980: 141) describe Garfinkel as "[A] young brilliant graduate student" who "wished to pursue the question of race and homicide further." At the time there were no official statistical data available that allowed to differentiate homicide by categorizing them as "black killing black, black killing white, white killing black, and white killing white" (Johnson and Johnson 1980: 140). Guy Johnson therefore encouraged Garfinkel to pursue his interest. Garfinkel then "assembled data from court records, coroners' reports, and newspapers on all homicides (in ten counties in central North Carolina) over a period of eleven years, by race, sex, and socioeconomic status of offenders and victims. He traced each indictment through the judicial possibilities: nol pros, acquittal, conviction, sentencing. ... All in all, Garfinkel made some of the most remarkable tabulations of criminal statistics ever compiled" (Johnson and Johnson 1980: 141). His statistical analysis confirmed Johnson's hypothesis and "left no doubt as to the reality of differentials in the administration of justice in terms of offender/victim categories of homicide" (Johnson and Johnson 1980: 141).

Garfinkel, however, did not stop with the statistical analysis but conducted "a personal and summary evaluation of actual trial situations" (1949: 376), which he witnessed in the courts that formed part of his statistical investigation. He saw court hearings as "magical and ritual" places that fulfill various functions that eventually allow "to either absolve the desecrator of his stain or to require that the stain be wiped out by appropriate punishment" (1949: 376). Their function was to identify offenses and offenders and to provide the prosecution with the means to use their authority to make decisions about the fate of the indicted person; s/he was either acquitted or convicted in order to restore social order in society (1949: 376).

His observations in the courts suggested that prosecutors and judges apply a certain reasoning that underpins the social order of the society of the day; "the processes of trial consist of activities oriented to the reinstatement of desecrated communally sanctioned values" (1949: 376). Thereby, Garfinkel was interested in the accounts that were given for prosecution and was able to at least give an indication of the regard courts pay to the four types of cases. His qualitative analysis of the courts' accounts allowed him to explain why offenses committed by African Americans against Whites were more often sentenced as "murder" than in comparable cases of the other three categories. The charge against an African American to have murdered a white person was the first step to restoring the white value system. The status of the act as "criminal" was already established at the beginning of the trial (Garfinkel 1949: 377). As the court hearing that often ended with the conviction for murder continued, "justice" as seen by the white community was done (Garfinkel 1949: 376, 378). The explanations given by judges and jurors when accounting for their decisions restored the social order of society that had been threatened by the criminal offense.

Because the number of cases in Garfinkel's collection was small, he was unable to conduct a similarly detailed analysis of incidents where white people were accused and convicted of the murder of African Americans. However, he did study in some detail offenses among Whites and offenses among African Americans. His analysis of the crime statistics showed that in cases of the indictment of African Americans, the accused were convicted for manslaughter, while in the same kind of indictments, Whites often received lesser sentences or were even acquitted (Garfinkel 1949: 370–375). Garfinkel furthermore observed in court that, in these cases, the murder charge was pragmatically made at the commencement of the court hearing (Garfinkel 1949: 380). It then became possible to arrive at a lesser charge and conviction later, while this procedure would not be possible at a hearing with a lesser charge at the beginning.

Differences in the procedure of court hearings where Whites and African Americans were being charged were based on the accounts that were given to determine the culpability of the accused (1949: 379). When white people were being charged, a court looked for reasons and motives for the offense; the white court could do this because it was familiar with the living conditions of the white population. Garfinkel claimed that in these cases

> the circumstances in the lives of white offenders are familiar, legitimately meaningful, acceptable or rejectable according to immediately understandable criteria, criteria which are closely circumscribed by traditional interpretive schemata, familiar in the lives of bonafide in-group members of a white moral community who had been doing business at the stand of trouble for a long time (Garfinkel 1949: 379).

The court, therefore, could make fine distinctions when legitimizing charges and convictions. Because of the marginal status of African

Americans and the contempt they faced in the white community (1949: 380), courts were not familiar with possible reasons and motives of the offenses that an African American had committed and the search for motives would be ridiculed (1949: 379). Therefore, when convicting a white person for an offense, his living conditions and possible motive were taken into consideration, while in the case of African Americans, a court convicted the offender for pragmatic reasons.

These different perspectives to people's actions that eventually had the same result, i.e., the death of another human being, led to fewer murder charges and convictions for accused Whites than African Americans. The jurisdiction argued that white people could be ascribed understandable motives for their offenses, while with African Americans, one just could not be sure why they committed a certain offense. Accounts for the convictions of African Americans who had killed a white person described the action as "heinously criminal" (1949: 378) and thus made the death penalty unproblematic.

Garfinkel's analysis was based on a perspective that considered charges and convictions as *accounts*, although Garfinkel was not yet using this term. This perspective allowed him to describe crime statistics in new ways and to reveal that these statistics were failing to represent the distribution of charges and convictions between White and African American accused. Instead, by taking this perspective, charges and convictions became descriptions of the social order that differentiated between white people and African American accused (1949: 378). Garfinkel's detailed observations in court, where convictions turned the accused into criminals, allowed him to begin to conceive social order in new ways. Rather than being an objective entity, Garfinkel regarded social order as an accomplishment of the participants in court, including judges, jurors, and prosecutors. A few years later, Garfinkel would take up studying the social order in court again, and ever since then, interaction in court has been of central concern to ethnomethodological and conversation analytic research (cf. Burns 2005; Dingwall 2000; Travers and Manzo 1997). So, already this early in his career, Garfinkel was examining in detail the relationship between an established social order and the ways in which people account for that social order. Such accounts can provide sociologists with an important resource to explain how actors in situations produce social order.

Johnson was very impressed with Garfinkel and his contribution to the project. He not only thanks Garfinkel in a publication (1941) that summarizes the key findings of the project but also encourages him to publish his master's thesis completed in 1942; "but Garfinkel, ever the perfectionist, hesitated to see it published" and it was not until after the war in 1949 that he summarized his study and published a paper on the research in *Social Forces* (Johnson and Johnson 1980: 141).

Aside from studying for a master's degree and participating in the research project directed by Johnson, Garfinkel also became interested in Gestalt psychology and Husserl's phenomenology. In fact, as Rawls (2002: 14) writes:

> [W]hile Burke's theory of accounts inspired Garfinkel to begin studying the social production of accounts, and William I. Thomas and Florian Znaniecki introduced him to the importance of the actor's point of view, it was the courses in phenomenology at North Carolina that led Garfinkel to consider the problem of recognizable patterns of social events.

Garfinkel studied Schutz's and Gurwitsch's works and explored how phenomenological concepts and ideas could be related to his sociological studies. In particular, he became interested in the observability and intelligibility of social action. Over the following years, he sharpened his perspective and turned his studies to the development of a specific sociological perspective and the problem of social order. What in 1939 had begun with a hitch-hike to North Carolina, where he took up studying sociology, arrived at its completion in 1942: Garfinkel successfully submitted his master's thesis. Now he was a sociologist.

# Chapter 3

# Sociology and *Sociological Attitude*

In December 1941 the USA entered World War II. When American troops were deployed to Europe, Garfinkel enlisted in the US Air Force. However, he was not sent abroad, but was given the task of training soldiers for tank combat in Europe. Without any tanks at his disposal to practice combat, he relied on the reports of war correspondents and photographs he found in magazines like *Life* when he prepared recruits for the war in Europe (Rawls 2002: 15). While in the air force Garfinkel continued his studies of phenomenology, reading Husserl's (2010) *Ideas: General Introduction to a Pure Phenomenonlogy* and Farber's (2006 [1943]) *The Foundation of Phenomenology*, as well as Schutz's (1945b) essay "On Multiple Realities" (Psathas 2009; Rawls 2002).

After the war, Garfinkel returned to his studies of sociology. He had his eyes set on Harvard, where Talcott Parsons was developing his theories of society and *social order*. As Parsons' doctoral student, and influenced by his intensive studies of phenomenology and his sociological training at Chapel Hill, Garfinkel began to explore Hobbes' problem of social order that underlay Parsons' work and started to develop his own sociological attitude, i.e., a way of sociologically studying · social order that fundamentally differed from that of Parsons and other contemporary (and now classic) sociologists.

In this chapter, I trace the development of Garfinkel's sociological perspective. I discuss in some detail a book recently edited by Anne Rawls entitled *Seeing Sociologically* (Garfinkel 2006 [1948]). This book is based on a manuscript Garfinkel wrote in the early stages of his PhD research. The detailed discussion of this book provides the background and basis for the exploration of Garfinkel's doctoral dissertation in the following chapter, and for understanding the particular *sociological attitude* that has remained the cornerstone of the sociology he created later in his career.

## The Department of Social Relations at Harvard

Garfinkel's decision to move to Harvard was based on contemporary developments of sociology as an academic discipline in the USA. While in post-war USA the Department of Sociology at the University of North Carolina was still of importance within sociology, more innovative and influential developments were happening at Harvard, where Talcott Parsons (Sociology), Gordon Allport (Psychology), and Clyde Kluckhohn (Social Anthropology) had founded the Department of Social Relations in 1946 (Homans 1984; Vidich 2000).

Parsons led the Department and shaped it to support his intellectual ambitions for the development of a general theory of the social system (Homans 1984; Vidich 2000).[1] From the start, Parsons understood that such a theoretical effort required interdisciplinarity. He therefore created an environment where the key figures in the various disciplines were intellectually and administratively linked. Thus, he hoped to be able to draw together and integrate the key theories and concepts from these disciplines and develop a common language for the social sciences (Vidich 2000). Parsons' efforts to create an interdisciplinary research center forged close connections between the Department of Social Relations, where he worked with Pitirim Sorokin, Samuel Stouffer, Robert Freed Bales, and George Caspar Homans; social anthropologists like Clyde Kluckhohn and Barrington Moore; psychologists like Gordon Allport, Richard Salomon, and Jerome Bruner; psychoanalysts like Edward G. Boring and the famous radical behaviorist Burrhus Frederic Skinner. The interdisciplinarity of the Department of Social Relations provided Parsons' students with a multitude and variety of perspectives and discussions in lectures and seminars (Homans 1984; Vidich 2000).

On Garfinkel's arrival at Harvard in 1948, the Department of Social Relations was still in the early stages of its development. He began his doctoral research with students who later became influential figures in American sociology, including Duncan MacRae, Bernard Barber, Frank Sutton, Fred Strodtbeck, Hans Lucas Täuber, and Arthur J. Vidich (Rawls 2007). In light of the theories and analyses that Parsons developed, Garfinkel was particularly interested in further exploring the question of social order. He also delved further into phenomenology and the analyses of Alfred Schutz's studies who, at the time, was teaching at the Graduate Faculty of the New School for Social Research in New York. Garfinkel used his reading of Husserl and Schutz to develop his specific sociological attitude and methods that would later allow him to investigate the question of social order from a novel perspective (Garfinkel 2002).

## Changing Perspectives: From Types to Practices

While at Harvard, Garfinkel discussed his ideas with Talcott Parsons as well as with Aron Gurwitsch and Alfred Schutz. These discussions helped Garfinkel to develop a novel perspective to address the question: "How is social order possible?" This question's origin is often ascribed to the English philosopher Thomas Hobbes (1588–1679) and is also seen as the foundational concern of sociology as a discipline. Sociological textbooks such as Giddens' (2009: xxi) *Sociology* return to this question when they discuss the reason for the emergence of sociology as an academic discipline and argue that "the transformations that wrenched the industrializing social order of the West away from the ways of life characteristic of preceding societies" led to the emergence of academic sociological debates.

Prior to the emergence of sociology as an academic discipline, numerous social philosophers like Hobbes and Jean-Jacques Rousseau (1712–1778) explored the "problem of social order" and the tensions between *egoism*, which keeps people apart and self-oriented and *altruism*, which encourages people to act for a greater societal good. The solution to this problem was either seen in a supreme power that keeps egoistical individuals in check (Hobbes) or in a "social contract" that people silently agree with and thus allow for a peaceful living together (Rousseau). These questions were taken up by the early, now classic, sociologists, such as Karl Marx, Emile Durkheim, Max Weber, and Georg Simmel, who explored society at the turn of the twentieth century as it was subjected to a changing economic and political landscape (Münch 1994).

Garfinkel had experienced the problems of social order first hand when growing up in a community marginal to the rest of US society: "Jews were not considered White and accommodations were often not open to them" (Rawls 2013: 308). He brought the marginality of his life experience in the 1930s to the fore, when writing his short story "Color Trouble" (Garfinkel 1940). When he moved to Harvard and joined Parsons' Department of Social Relations as a doctoral student, Garfinkel threw himself fully into the exploration of social order as a sociological question. Although at this stage he had not decided how to address the question, he already understood that it needed to be rephrased. He proposed developing a way to explore the question by considering social order as a concrete phenomenon, a "social fact" in Durkheim's sense that participants in social situations continuously generate in and through their actions (Rawls 2002, 2003). His concern, therefore, was to understand the participants' perspective of social situations (Psathas 2004; Rawls 2007).

Parsons and Schutz addressed the sociological question of *social order* in two ways: First, they conceived it as a problem of sociological description, i.e., they explored ways in which it was possible to investigate and then describe appropriately, or in Schutz's (1943) terminology "adequately", the social world actors inhabit. Second, they conducted largely theoretical studies of the social world to understand and describe its social order. Both Schutz and Parsons took Max Weber's ([1948]1998) concept of *social action* as the starting-point for their studies and the question of how the social sciences could arrive at historically comparable data and scientifically founded propositions or descriptions. For this purpose, Weber developed the concept of *ideal types* and differentiated four types of action: goal-rational, value-rational, traditional, and affectual. These ideal types are theoretical types or analytic categories that cannot be found in reality. In Weber's sense, these analytic types were constructed to help sociologists differentiate and describe social phenomena and compare them over time. They can be deployed for intercultural and historical comparisons of societies and social arrangements.

Parsons largely agreed with Weber's arguments (1937). He also was convinced that sociologists required analytic tools to study social order in an otherwise seemingly disorganized social world. However, Parsons considered Weber's ideal types as insufficient for sociologists to make historically comparable propositions on the relationship between actor and situation. He developed a complex scheme of distinctions that, taken together, could be used to capture and analytically describe how the actor orients to the situation. This scheme of distinctions, known as *pattern variables*, (Parsons 1951; Parsons 1960; Parsons and Shils 1952) is comprised of a system of five contrast pairs: affectivity and affective neutrality; self-orientation and collective-orientation; universalism and particularism; ascription and achievement; and specificity and diffusion. The sociologist can use these pattern variables to interpret the relationship between an actor, such as a human individual, an institution, or a cultural system, with situations.[2] They can be understood as Parsons' attempt to develop an analytical concept that sociologists could deploy to systematically investigate actors' orientation to a situation (Münch 1981, 1982).

Thus, Parsons' pattern variables are a system of general categories that sociologists can use to describe the social world from the point of view of the researcher who uses this analytic scheme. They are an analytic tool for social scientists to see order in a world that from their social-scientific perspective looks contingent and unintelligible and which therefore a sociologist would find difficult to "objectively" describe in a traditional sense of the word. As we have seen above with Weber, the analytic base of these categories enables sociologists to arrive at historically and interculturally comparable descriptions of the social world. Yet the comparability of the social-scientific descriptions of the situation is tied to the scheme of distinctions deployed by the researcher and therefore differs from the way in which the actor orients to the situation.

Schutz was critical of analytic systems such as the ones proposed by Weber and Parsons. From a phenomenological perspective he argued that such theoretical concepts failed to understand actors' orientation and experience of the social world (Endress 2009). He suggested that Parsons' theory did not resolve the problem of adequate sociological descriptions of social situations, i.e., the relationship between analytic descriptions and people's experience of the social world. Schutz therefore proposed to differentiate between the perspective of the actor; the perspective of the observer in the everyday; and the perspective of the social scientific observer (Schutz 1953), or in his words, "first order constructs," "second order constructs," and "third order constructs." By deploying this phenomenological method, Schutz (1945a&b) interpreted the processes through which the actor in the everyday produces meaningful action, thus addressing Weber and Parsons' failure to provide methods to understand the actor's point of view. In other words, Schutz's argument implied a critique of Parsons' failure to see "that a theory of social action primarily has to answer questions concerning the 'pragmatic constitution of the social person' and its intersubjective framing and interrelation" (Endress 2009: 387). Or, to use Schutz's words:

> [N]owhere in your theory do you deal with the specific social categories of acting and mutual interaction, with the problem of the frame of reference relative to the alter ego towards which the actor's own actions are oriented and within which the alter ego interprets the actor's action (Schutz in Grathoff 1978: 104 in Endress 2009: 387).[3]

Schutz proposed to analyze social order by shedding the reliance on analytic categories created by social scientists and instead elaborating on the types that actors themselves use when they make sense of situations. He particularly concerned himself with Weber's concept of *ideal types* and revised it in such a way that it could be used to understand the actor's point of view and actors' use of typologies of objects, events, actions etc. in concrete situations. Schutz argued that while people might encounter unfamiliar situations, they were still able to act and interact in them by using such actor-generated typologies. In his studies, therefore, these actor-generated typologies replaced the normative basis that underlay Parsons' pattern variables and concept of social order. While Parsons had argued that actors' actions are based on internalized norms, Schutz, according to Endress (2009: 387), "insists on the difference between intersubjective norms and their subjective internalization or appropriation."

While Parsons had removed social scientists from the perspective of the everyday to adopt a perspective where sociologists could produce historically comparable propositions by deploying a general analytic system, Schutz's sociology remained on the level of the everyday. He argued that like the actor in social situations, sociologists rely on typologies to describe the everyday. In this view, sociologists create and use second order constructions to analyze the structures of the everyday. The propositions derived from this perspective remain "adequate" because they are not based on general theories, concepts, and categories like Parsons' pattern variables; rather, they directly relate to the typologies that actors use in concrete situations.

The difference between Parsons' and Schutz's perspectives becomes apparent when considering the different ways in which the two scholars considered the relationship between norms, rules, and action. While Parsons regarded norms and rules as a basis for action, Schutz viewed them as a resource that actors develop when they deploy typologies of situations. Schutz proposed to take into account the subjective perspective of the actor and to explore the motives that actors use when orienting to and acting in situations. He argued that meaning in situations was contingent and subject to continuous change, constituted in the "here and now." By adopting this perspective developed by Schutz, it becomes problematic to generate objective propositions concerned with the social scientific understanding of actions. Schutz therefore developed a keen interest in further exploring the question of adequate social scientific descriptions of the everyday that were also historically comparable.

In his book *Phenomenology of the Social World* (Schutz 1967b [1932]) and in the posthumously published *Structures of the Life World* (Schutz and Luckmann 1974) Schutz developed a terminology to characterize the perspective he suggested sociologists should adopt, including concepts of spatial, temporal, and social distance; the biographical situation; the elements of the stock of knowledge; subjective system of relevances; the reciprocity of perspectives; and congruency of relevance systems that are designed to address such issues. Like Parsons, Schutz was primarily concerned with the development of a *matrix* (Luckmann 1973; Eberle 1984, 2008; Eberle and Hitzler 2000) that could be used to explicate the invariant everyday structures of the life-world.

## Garfinkel's *Sociological Attitude*

In 1948, Garfinkel wrote a manuscript entitled "Prospectus for an exploratory study of communicative effort and the modes of understanding in selected types of dyadic relationships." At the time of writing the text, Garfinkel was aware of the risk that his concept of social order might be likened to the then-influential behaviorist theories developed by John B. Watson since the late nineteenth century and Burrhus F. Skinner, who was one of the key members of the Department of Social Relations at Harvard when Garfinkel took up his studies there. He therefore refrained from using the term "interaction" in the title of the manuscript and replaced it with "communication" to ensure the relationships between the actions he described were not seen as driven by a stimulus-response mechanism (Rawls 2006).

The manuscript was an attempt by Garfinkel to formulate a plan for his doctoral dissertation. In the end, he never came to write *this* doctoral dissertation and the manuscript remained unpublished for decades. Only a few students and colleagues, such as Erving Goffman and Harvey Sacks, read and commented on the text before its publication by Anne Rawls in 2006 with the title *Seeing Sociologically.*

In *Seeing Sociologically*, Garfinkel developed a specific *sociological attitude* for sociologists to deploy when analyzing social reality. This attitude rendered Schutz's differentiation of natural attitude and scientific attitude superfluous. In a letter to Schutz, Garfinkel mentioned his manuscript titled "Notes on the sociological attitude" (Psathas 2004: 17) that seems to bear similarities to *Seeing Sociologically*. In the letter, Garfinkel explained how, in his view, the manuscript was based on Schutz's writings, in particular his essay "On Multiple Realities" (Schutz 1945b). Schutz responded to Garfinkel in a letter in which he agreed with the then young student concerning the differentiation between natural and scientific attitude (Psathas 2004: 17). He also liked the concept of a sociological attitude that Garfinkel developed in the manuscript, but would have preferred to call it "the attitude of the sociologist" (Schutz in Psathas 2004: 17). Schutz encouraged Garfinkel in his studies by describing the study of the practical decision making and the methods used by the sociologist to uncover them as an "undiscovered treasure island" (Psathas 2009: 423–424), a field of research that promised interesting findings.

Garfinkel recognized Schutz's efforts to adequately describe the social world from the actor's perspective. However he argued that Schutz's as well as Parsons' studies would not allow the sociologist to describe social reality from the actor's point of view. They both relied on the distinction between the social scientist and the everyday actor's perspective. Therefore, in the end, they would both arrive at descriptions of social reality from a sociologist's perspective that fundamentally differs from that of the actor in actual situations. He considered Parsons' approach as reliant on the view that the application of rational, scientific methods would make social scientific descriptions superior to the viewpoint and description offered by the everyday perspective. In Parsons' view, Garfinkel suggested, social scientists would need to further develop and improve their methods of analysis and description, but basically they were on the right track.

Schutz challenged Parsons by highlighting the differences between the social and natural sciences and argued for a shift in focus that required social scientists to explore the social world from the perspective of the everyday actor. By drawing on Husserl's phenomenology, Schutz explicated how the "attitude" or "cognitive style" (Schutz 1945b) that actors adopt in concrete situations defined actions produced in the everyday. The specific cognitive style, Schutz argued, was brought to bear by actors in a situation and thus defined how they oriented to, experienced, and acted in that situation (Schutz 1945b). For Schutz the *postulate of adequacy* demanded that

> [E]ach term in a scientific model of human action must be construct-
> ed in such a way that a human act performed within the life-world
> by an individual actor in the way indicated by the typical construct
> would be understandable for the actor himself as well as for his fel-
> low-men in terms of common-sense interpretation of everyday life
> (Schutz 1943, 1945b).

Garfinkel (2006 [1948]) was dissatisfied with Schutz's concept of adequate description and his approach of exploring social order, or as Schutz and Luckmann (1974) later called it "The structure of the life-world." In his view, Schutz's approach still implied a superiority of the scientific perspective over the perspective of the everyday actor. Garfinkel argued that Schutz was unable to explain how to understand the relationship between everyday and scientific descriptions. As this relationship remained unexplained by Schutz, he would ultimately produce social scientific descriptions that necessarily differed from the ways in which actors in concrete situations would experience and make sense of them (Eberle 2008).

Garfinkel (2006 [1948]) suggested that the scientific and natural attitudes to the everyday were fundamentally different. Actors in the everyday would conduct themselves in situations by pragmatically de-ploying a particular *cognitive style* and a pragmatic orientation to the task in hand, while social scientists were concerned with producing scientific descriptions of the everyday.[4] In Garfinkel's view, Schutz was trying to use the analysis of the life-world to develop concepts that so-cial scientists could use to interpret the actor's perspective in situations. As far as Garfinkel was concerned, this concept of social scientific anal-yses was not radical enough because, like Parsons' pattern variables, Schutz's analysis of the life-world was based on generic categories that formed the basis for social scientific descriptions. These descriptions idealized the everyday rather than helping understand the actual natural attitude that actors bring to bear in concrete situations.

Garfinkel accepted that Parsons and Schutz had developed very interesting and innovative ways to understand the social order of the everyday. However, he suggested radicalizing their positions further in order to arrive at truly adequate descriptions of the everyday. For this purpose, it was necessary for both scholars to give up the assumption that scientific descriptions were superior to everyday descriptions, because such a position would inevitably lead to idealizations that differed from practices in the everyday. Furthermore, the generation of generic categories, classifications and typologies was grounded in the specifics of the orientation that they adopted when developing such concepts. Hence, it was impossible to arrive at historically comparable propositions: "[...] there are still ontological elements in the meanings of the structures he [Schutz] proposed—in this case a scientific ontology—which would mean in turn that the break with ethnocentrism had been incomplete" (Garfinkel 2006 [1948]: 137). Garfinkel argued that social scientists could only overcome this problem by giving up the scientific idealization of the everyday (Garfinkel 2006 [1948]: 135–137); the social scientist would need to look for the social order of the everyday in the actors' practical actions, rather than in concepts of the order of actions.

Garfinkel conducted his discussion of Parsons and Schutz in order to develop a specific sociological attitude that social scientists could use to describe social reality. He suggested avoiding scientific idealizations of the everyday and producing descriptions of the everyday that, at the same time, had a scientific character and were viewed as adequate by the participants. Such descriptions therefore needed to be based on the *cognitive style* that the actors in the situation adopt when "working" in the everyday (Garfinkel 2006 [1948]: 132–145). In Garfinkel's view it was only possible to produce such descriptions when the researcher embedded him/herself (as far as possible) in the situation. Thus s/he would be able to acquire and appropriate the knowledge and competencies that actors deploy in the everyday. For Garfinkel, therefore, it was necessary for the sociologist to adopt the orientation and attitude of the participant in the situation so that the embodied knowledge of the participant became intelligible for her/him. Attempts to deploy a scientific orientation and attitude as well as scientific techniques, such as typologies and classifications, to make sense of the everyday could not succeed.[5]

Garfinkel therefore rejected the assumption that participants' natural attitude could be reconstructed by deploying a scientific attitude. He argued that social scientists relied on such a scientific attitude when they were describing everyday situations based on theoretical constructs derived from a scientific attitude. In his view, social scientists worked with the presupposition that social scientific theories and methods would allow them to produce objective descriptions. Yet such an approach to the description of the everyday created myths and theories that already existed in society. Garfinkel further suggested that social scientists often treated social reality just like everyday actors who also relied on theories and methods (Psathas 2009). Therefore, social scientific descriptions that were not grounded in a sociological attitude, i.e., an attitude based on the lived experience of the situation, remained "inadequate" (Rawls 2006: 92, Fn. 11). For Garfinkel, the critical question was how the sociological attitude could be deployed to create descriptions of the everyday that the actors themselves could treat as *adequate*.

Garfinkel therefore suggested that sociologists should give up conventional methods of analysis and adopt a different perspective on the everyday that allows for the production of adequate descriptions of the everyday. He later characterized the requirement for descriptions based on this sociological attitude as *unique adequacy* (Garfinkel and Wieder 1992). The unique adequacy postulate "radicalized" (Eberle 1984) Schutz's proposition to prioritize the perspective of the actors in social situation when producing descriptions of the everyday. Unique adequacy implied that it was insufficient to imaginatively take the perspective of the actor, as argued by symbolic interactionists and others. Instead, it was necessary for the researcher to practically undertake, and thus understand, the actors' actions. When Garfinkel talked about the *sociological attitude* he was talking about more than an intellectual change of perspectives. In this sociological attitude he saw a fundamentally different concept of sociology in general, and the sociology of knowledge in particular. It therefore is wrong to subsume Garfinkel and ethnomethodology under the interpretivist research tradition, as many commentators and textbooks have done (Denzin 1969; Rogers 1983). In later chapters, I pursue Garfinkel's development of his sociology. In the remainder of this chapter, I explore Garfinkel's proposal to change the sociological approach to study society by investigating his studies of the "phenomenon of social order."

## The Phenomenon of Social Order

Garfinkel developed the notion of sociological attitude by examining the theories of Parsons, Schutz and pragmatism[6], as well as other contemporary approaches. The study of these theories and approaches to sociology allowed him to develop the program of research that later became known as *ethnomethodology*. Therewith, Garfinkel conceived *social order* in a way that fundamentally differed from that pervading large parts of sociology. In his view, "[t]he term 'social order' is a title for the problem of permanence and change as they are relevant to the work day investigations and theorizings of social scientists" (Garfinkel 1952: 5).

In sociology, however, social order had only been treated as a theoretical problem. Parsons, for example, argued that in society the problem of social order was resolved by the existence of norms and values that people acquired through socialization and education (Parsons 1951). Schutz, by contrast, proposed shifting the argument from a normative order of the social world to an order based on knowledge. In his view, therefore, sociologists should explore different forms of knowledge, as well as its distribution and use in social situations. In a cognate way, Mead (1934) and Blumer (1969), the founders of symbolic interactionism, considered social order to be based on social interaction. In their view, social order was achieved when actors took the perspective of the other, thus creating a shared definition of the situation. In this view, social order became a reality lodged only in actors' heads.

Garfinkel argued that Parsons and Schutz, as well as the interactionists and Goffman, maintained a scientific perspective that was not suitable to describe social order as it was practically produced by actors in concrete situations. He reasoned that sociological theories implied that the social world was without order and that social scientific concepts and methods were required to make order observable and intelligible. Instead, in *Seeing Sociologically*, Garfinkel (2006 [1948]) proposed that actions were organized and orderly and therefore intelligible to others. In this view, social order exists in the social world independently from the social scientific observer and is produced in and through participants' actions. He argued that in order to understand how participants produce social order, it is necessary to analyze the *details of the production of action*. Garfinkel, therefore, was concerned with the *production* and *accomplishment* of situated practices and with how participants were able to orient in an intelligible way to each other's action. He suggested that through the design and production of their action, participants display a commitment to the situation at hand that allows others to bestow trust in them and the situation. And based on this trust in the other's commitment and competence, participants align their actions with each other and are able to ongoingly produce social order (Garfinkel 2008 [1952]; Heritage 1984; Watson 2009).

Garfinkel argued that the coherence of a situation was based on the knowledge and competency that allowed actors to act in specific situations in such a way that participants see actions as suitable and in alignment with the emerging context.[7] In order to competently act in social situations, actors are required to expend effort that generates mutually recognizable and intelligible social situations. This *communicative effort* is comprised of publicly observable exchanges of intelligible bodily and oral actions. It is based not only on a social order that exists prior to the actions, but is also the location where the social order becomes observable in and through the accomplishment and organization of actions. Furthermore, communicative effort involves not only bodily and oral action, but also material and tangible action. Hence, the term *interactional effort* appears to capture the "work" that participants invest in social situations. However, Garfinkel refrained from using the term "interaction" in his 1948 manuscript, because the term was tainted by the contemporary behaviorists' research he was aiming to distance his project from.

In Garfinkel's view, interaction work was *sequentially organized*, making the meaning of actions observable and intelligible. By *sequence* he was not referring to the temporally organized process of actions, their serial occurrence, but to the meaningful interrelationship between actions. He argued that actions acquire their meaning by orienting to prior and subsequent actions at the same time (Rawls 2006: 29–41). By virtue of the accomplishment of actions, actors confirm their understanding of the prior action and prepare the basis for subsequent actions (Garfinkel 2006 [1948]).[8] Interpretations of actions, therefore, are not objects lodged in people's heads, but are made observable by each subsequent action designed so that co-participants are able to recognize its relationship to the prior action and are able to produce the next action. Thus, each action becomes, as noted by Garfinkel (2006 [1948]: 180), an "experiment in miniature," whose success is instantiated by the co-participant's next action.[9] And the meaning of each action arises only in and through the next action.

The concept of *communicative effort* or *interactional effort,* already developed by Garfinkel (2006 [1948]) prior to the completion of his doctoral dissertation, has implications for the sociological approach to *meaning* and *intersubjectivity*, as well as for the methods through which sociologists investigate social order. The meaning of actions and objects is accomplished in and through actions. It is not the product of cognitive processes, but a practical achievement generated by actors who deploy a "natural attitude" in specific situations. Intersubjectivity, therefore, is not a presupposition of social interaction, but is a practical achievement produced in and through participants' actions, as and when they are accomplished.[10] The understanding of action and social

order cannot be derived from interviews with the actors who participated in a situation rather, as far as possible, the sociologist needs to become a member of the actual situation. Garfinkel criticized interview-
based research for relying on the assumption that the interviewee was
the same person who acted in the situation the interviewer questioned
her/him about. Instead, he had already argued in 1948 that identity
was coupled to specific situations and emerging actions. The actor who
acts in a situation is a different person than the interviewee, because
the cognitive style s/he deploys in the interview differs from the cognitive style used in the situation under scrutiny. In Garfinkel's view, the
perspectives of actors are linked to the specifics of the situation and
cannot be recovered through interviews. He emphasized his argument
by drawing on the case of the guard of the main entrance to a library
whose *identity* as a guard is not based on the attribution of a particular
role with given properties, but on his actions that make others treat
him as the guard of the library (Garfinkel 2006 [1948]: 110–114). What
makes the man a library guard cannot be reconstructed through interviews about his work, thus the sociologist needs to understand the
practices that in specific circumstances make observable and intelligible that the man is the guard of the library.

Garfinkel's sociological perspective and focus on the situatedness
of practices entailed a revision of key sociological concepts, such as
*role* and *group*.[11] Contemporary sociologists like Linton (1936) attributed particular characteristics and motives that define their actions
to actors. They argued that this attribution allowed actors to "take the
role of the other" in social situations. This concept of role is based on
the assumption that motives and plans are characteristics actors have
internalized and bring with them when entering situations. Garfinkel, however, suggested that role identities are practical achievements
continuously accomplished in and through the production of actions.
They are not properties of people, but products of interactional effort.[12]
In the same way, Garfinkel described groups as situated assemblies of
actors that are maintained as long as participants deploy their actions
in ways which display that they mutually orient to the situation in the

same way. Thereby, actors deploy a cognitive style such that their actions become observable and intelligible as group actions.

Social order, identity, role, and group are practical achievements. They are accomplished in and through participants' actions that become intelligibly observable as coherent and meaningful. In *Seeing Sociologically*, Garfinkel (2006 [1948]) developed the basis for his program of research that he later called *ethnomethodology*. At the time of his development of ideas about the need to respecify key sociological concepts, Garfinkel was strongly influenced by his intellectual engagement with Schutz and phenomenology. This engagement with Schutz's social phenomenology is reflected in Garfinkel's doctoral dissertation that he submitted to Harvard in 1952.[13]

# From Phenomenology
# to Ethnomethodology

When Garfinkel began his doctoral studies at Harvard he was occupied with the question of the possibility of *social order* and with developing an analytic and methodological framework to approach the question from the perspective of the actor. He had rejected concepts that conceived of social order as a cognitive process lodged in actors' heads. Yet he also was sensitive to the risk that if he were to focus his research on action, his studies might be seen and criticized for being behaviorist (Garfinkel 2006 [1948]). He believed that sociologists could examine the basis for social order and devised a research project for his doctoral dissertation to pursue this interest. For the purpose of the project he continued his analysis of Parsons' and Schutz's concepts of the social world. In this chapter, I discuss Garfinkel's doctoral dissertation in some detail and investigate its contribution to the later development of ethnomethodology (cf. Koschmann 2012a).

As a doctoral student of Talcott Parsons, Garfinkel studied at the Department of Social Relations in Harvard, where the future of social scientific research was seen in the deployment of surveys and statistical methods to gather and analyze data. To obtain approval for his doctoral research project, Garfinkel was relying on the support of Parsons and of the PhD examination committee at Harvard. It would have been unwise for the still-young sociologist to propose a project that solely used research methods and techniques that his doctoral advisor or the eminent scientific community at Harvard would not approve. He chose the statistician Frederick Mosteller as his second doctoral advisor and began a research project that, through experimental methods, produced statistical data he then subjected to careful analysis. The well-known so-

*Harold Garfinkel: The Creation and Development of Ethnomethodology* by Dirk vom Lehn. 57–78. © 2013 UVK Verlagsgesellschaft mbH; additional material for English edition © 2014 Left Coast Press, Inc. All rights reserved.

cial scientist, Samuel Stouffer (1906–1960), then Director of the laboratories of the Department of Social Relations, allowed Garfinkel access to the facilities and supported him in the experiments. Thus, Garfinkel not only made use of the departmental facilities, but also gained the support of key figures in the Department whom he would need to successfully complete his unusual doctoral research project (Rawls 2002).

## Theory of Correspondence and Theory of Congruence

Aside from his PhD advisors and the support in the Department, Garfinkel remained in close contact with Alfred Schutz and Aron Gurwitsch throughout his doctoral research. In evening seminars in New York, Garfinkel discussed with them the phenomenological questions that he addressed in his research. Garfinkel arrived at the conclusion that it was critical to first develop a sound sociological perspective before embarking on his research project. He was convinced that whatever perspective he chose for his project would also determine its results and implications. Hence, Garfinkel's PhD dissertation began with an extensive explanation of the viewpoints that Parsons and Schutz deployed in their work when exploring the question of social order. Starting with this discussion, Garfinkel developed his own perspective that formed the basis for the experiments he conducted and analyzed as part of his dissertation (Garfinkel 1952).

Garfinkel argued that Parsons and Schutz proposed two fundamentally different concepts of social science in their analysis of social reality. It is worthwhile remembering here that in the 1930s, sociology was still a young discipline and sociologists, therefore, worked hard to differentiate their theories and research from psychology, history, economics, and political science. Durkheim's (1982 [1895]) *The Rules of Sociological Method*, for example, can be read as a book that differentiates sociology from psychology by providing a framework for an empirical social science. In *The Structure of Social Action* Parsons (1937) contributed to these debates. Although in this book he developed a voluntaristic[1] theory in a review of Schelting's (1934) book on Max Weber's (1998 [1948]) *Methodology of Social Sciences,* Parsons highlighted that, "there is a methodological core common to all empirical science, no matter what its concrete subject matter" (Parsons in Heritage 1984: 19). Furthermore, he advocated a social science that produced "generalized laws characteristic of natural science" (Heritage 1984: 19). His subsequent theoretical developments, therefore, should be seen as advances in the "construction of a sociological science" (Heritage 1984: 20). For this purpose, Parsons developed his *pattern variables* (Parsons 1960; Parsons and Shils 1952) as a general analytic scheme that could be used to analyze actors' "subjective" orientations to a given situation and to make the findings of this analysis comparable. Parsons deployed this analytic classification scheme in the hope that it would enable him to develop a theoretical basis for the social sciences (Heritage 1984: 20).

From here on, the question arose for Parsons to explain how subjective value orientations, as described by the pattern variables, could be aligned to enable the emergence of social order. As he further developed his theoretical work, Parsons' response to the question of social order was that actors would internalize value patterns that guide or determine their action. In Parsons' theory, therefore, social order is the product of a system of values external to, but lodged in, the minds of actors. Actors have no influence on these values, but internalize and act in response to them (Heritage 1984: 22). In his *Studies* Garfinkel (1967b: ix) praised Parsons' work and described it as, "awesome for the penetrating depth and unfailing precision of its practical sociological reasoning on the constituent tasks of the problem of social order and its solutions." Later in *Studies*, however, Garfinkel sharply criticized the Parsonian framework without providing detailed theoretical arguments against it. Such a critical assessment of Parsons' work, however, can be found in his PhD dissertation.

In his dissertation Garfinkel differentiated between two distinct theoretical perspectives that at the time of his writing were deployed by social scientists, namely the *theory of congruity* adopted by Schutz and the *theory of correspondence* adopted by Parsons. Before turning to

Garfinkel's discussion of Schutz's proposal to study social reality, I first explore Parsons' approach. The theory of correspondence that underpins Parsons' work implies a fundamental, not-removable difference between the experienced object and the concrete object (Garfinkel 1952: 93). In Memo #3 published in *Toward a Sociological Theory of Information* Garfinkel (2008[1952]: 126) writes:

> The correspondence theory makes a separation between the real world and the subjective interpretation of the real world. The separation is such that there are on the one hand concrete objects in all their fullness and on the other a conceptual representation of these objects, which in abstracting certain features from them presents the scientist with a faded reproduction.

In this view, the observer is never able to grasp the concrete object, i.e., the Kantian "Ding-an-sich," because the perception and description of the world rely on systems of reference that organize the world (Münch 1981, 1982). These analytic categories, theories, and concepts never entirely match reality, but necessarily remain approximations. By using rational-scientific methods, the observer is able to come very close to, but never quite achieve, descriptions that are congruent with reality. Such scientific descriptions use language, signs, and symbols to represent reality in a way that comes as close to reality as possible. Parsons regarded these scientific descriptions that are derived by using rational-scientific methods as superior to the accounts produced by actors in the everyday. For example, in his view, the social scientist can use research methods and thereupon differentiate the character of actions as *rational, affectual, traditional,* or *habitual.* Thereby, in Parsons' view, the use of rational-scientific methods guarantees the validity of the scientific descriptions of action.

When developing his social-scientific perspective Parsons started with the assumption that there is only one reality that the scientific observer and the everyday actor grasp in different ways, because they use different methods when approaching it. Both their perspectives of the world exist independently from each other, yet in Parsons' theory, the world-view of the scientific observer comes closer to reality than the perspective of the actor, which is unspecified and varied; in other words, "messy." Thus, the scientific perspective of the social world is a better approximation of it than the one deployed by the actor in the everyday. Parsons developed a (rational-scientific) framework that allowed the social scientist to bring order to the "messiness" of the social world. This framework was designed to answer the question of "how is social order possible?"

The example of Parsons' concept of *social order* is a good place from which to start to understand Garfinkel's (1952) critique of Parsons' social-scientific perspective. With regard to the possibility of social order in the everyday, Parsons suggested beginning with the assumption that a mechanism is required that aligns the diverging perspectives of everyday actors. He implied that without such a mechanism to precede the emergence of cooperation, it is impossible to understand how actors are able to avoid conflict. The mechanism that Parsons saw at work in social relationships is a "shared symbolic system" (Parsons 1951; Parsons and Shils 1952) to which actors mutually orient, while expecting others to do the same.

Garfinkel's (1952; Heritage 1984: 7–74) critique of Parsons' concept was principally threefold: First, in his view, the preference for scientifically rational action over the production of reasonable, mundane action in ordinary circumstances led to an understanding of social situations defined by shared norms and values. Second, Parsons' assumption that the internalization of norms and values defines social action stood in contradiction to the perfectly reasonable and rational accounts people themselves gave when explaining actions they had conducted in particular situations. Third, even if there were a shared symbolic system of norms and values, it would not be able to define how actions were conducted. In Memo #3 published in *Toward a Sociological Theory of Information*, Garfinkel also highlights that because in the view of the correspondence theory the scientific observer preselects features he will look for in the world he risks becoming "a mute observer who can see the concrete object but cannot tell what it is" (2008 [1952]: 127).

Because Parsons prioritized the scientific over the actor's perspective, he described the actor's subjective point of view by using objective categories. He "reconstructs the experiences of the actor by utilizing 'subjective categories' such as 'end', 'means', and 'conditions'" (Hama 2009: 441). Garfinkel (1952: 100), on the other hand, argued that the scientific observer would need to look inside actors' heads to identify their motives. In doing so, he drew on Schutz's phenomenological analyses, which suggested that "[A]ll normative values [...] are interpretable as systems of in-order-to or because motives, to the extent that the subjective point of view of all these phenomena is retained" (Grathoff 1978: 35–36 in Hama 2009: 441). The in-order-to motives, i.e., the ends and goals of action, are only available to the actor who is not identical with the observer. Schutz's (1945b) argument about the relationship between normative values and the system of in-order-to and because motives therefore implies an understanding that there are multiple realities, including the world of the actor and the world of the scientific observer. In the aforementioned Memo #3, Garfinkel (2008 [1952]: 129) writes: "The question for this theory, then, is not one, as it is in the correspondence theory, of what is the objective world and what is objective knowledge, but is rather, what are the varieties of objective worlds and what are the varieties of objective knowledge."

In his doctoral dissertation Garfinkel (1952: 117) explained the differences between the perspectives deployed by Parsons and Schutz by using the example of a person who wished to travel as quickly as possible from Harvard Square to Park Street in Cambridge (Massachusetts). How could it be explained that the actor decided to walk rather than travel by subway? Parsons would argue that the actor would gather information about the possible ways of traveling between the two locations and base her/his rational decision on this information. If the actor arrived at a decision that contradicts the rational, scientific criteria, then this would be attributed to her/his ignorance and irrational features in the process that led her/him to the decision. The rational decision would be to use the subway as it takes the least time.

In Parsons' phenomenology, therefore, "a community between the actor and the observer" (Garfinkel 1952: 110–111) is possible because, in principle, the actor can rely on the same rational methods that the observer deploys. By contrast, in Schutz's view, such a community between the actor and observer is not possible, because an actor facing such a situation would not deploy "objective" criteria, but rather her/his own rationalities to arrive at a decision about which route to take. In other words, the actor in the Schutzian phenomenology acts within the *natural attitude*, while the observer brings to bear the attitude of the scientist, which fundamentally differs from that of the actor and is designed to produce *second order* descriptions of the everyday. Therefore, while Parsons' scientific observer would consider the decision to walk as "irrational," Schutz proposed to examine the mundane knowledge and competences the actor uses when making the decision, without, however, giving up the distinction between first order and second order descriptions.

For Parsons there was only one reality. Together with Edward Shils, Parsons (1952: 103) therefore argued that "a book is primarily a cultural or symbolic object, not the paper, ink, and covers, which primarily makes the book into an object of orientation." Within his theoretical framework, the common view of a book as a cultural object is guaranteed by the normative standardization of culture. The intersubjectivity and shared knowledge implied in this framework are facilitated by communication that uses a common system of symbols. The meaning of things, therefore, is fixed and socially agreed upon prior to the emergence of social situations and it is embodied through language that maintains a correspondence between names and things (Heritage 1984: 29).

Garfinkel highly valued Parsons' work and praised it in his *Studies* as well as in other writings, such as the unpublished manuscript *Parsons' Primer* (Garfinkel 1960). Yet he had fundamental reservations about Parsons' view that the scientific perspective and scientific knowledge about the social world was superior to that of the actor. In Garfinkel's view, Parsons' argument that "knowledge is evaluated in terms of its agreement with the 'facts of the situation' as determined by the scientific observer" (Heritage 1984: 29) was flawed and needed to be corrected to capture social order as it presents itself to actors in the social world. In Memo #3 (2008 [1952]: 127) he argued that such a social-scientific perspective "can easily lead to something that might be called the fallacy of imposed order."

For the correction of Parsons' concept of the relationship between actor and situation Garfinkel (1952) drew on Schutz's social phenomenology. He (1952: 97) proposed to call Schutz's perspective a *theory of congruency*. From this perspective, the way in which an object is perceived and experienced is what the object is for the perceiver in this very moment; the experienced object and concrete object are the same. Therefore, different observers may see the world in different ways. The result is a "plurality of worlds" (Garfinkel 1952: 97) with people acting with different attitudes, motivations, etc. From this perspective a book has different meanings for different people in different situations. As Schutz said, in response to Parsons' suggestions that people, having internalized norms and values, would see a "book" as a cultural and symbolic object: "[N]ot for the bibliophile or librarian or bookseller" (Schutz in Endress 2009: 382). Within this framework, therefore, there is not one reality but *multiple realities* (Schutz 1945b) and multiple meanings of objects, people, and action that are constituted by deploying particular attitudes and orientations to the world.

Schutz's analyses were concerned with exploring how, in the social world, actors constitute objects on the basis of their knowledge about them and the relevance these objects have for them in specific situations. He investigated actors' orientation to the world as well as the shared *stock of knowledge* and the *system of relevances* they bring to bear in creating an intersubjective experience of the world (Schutz 1945b). He took into consideration that situations vary in their organization and require actors to quickly realize how to act within them. While Parsons had argued that situations are defined a priori based on a shared cultural value system and internalized norms, Schutz highlighted the contingency of situations and the inevitability of the contingency of shared understanding. Social order, therefore, becomes a cognitive problem that Schutz referred to when suggesting that actors deploy types and typologies to make sense of, and act in, contingent circumstances. These typologies reflect the knowledge actors use to produce, maintain, define, and question the organization of a shared order (Garfinkel 1952: 114).

Because people's ability to act in the social world relies on knowledge of that world, social scientists who use the theory of congruency investigate the structuring of people's experience of the social world. Schutz provided a framework to study the stock of knowledge and system of relevances that actors deploy in particular circumstances. Rather than beginning with assumptions about the rationality of actions, Schutz was concerned with the organization of the stock of knowledge and with how this stock of knowledge becomes observable and intelligible in the social world. In this theoretical framework, rationality is not only a property of science but also of the everyday itself. Because the rationality of the everyday fundamentally differs from the scientific rationality, the perspective of a social scientific observer is unsuitable for understanding how actors themselves experience the everyday (Schutz 1943).

Garfinkel (1952) recognized the advances that Schutz's theoretical analyses provided for the social scientist interested in understanding how actors experience and generate an intersubjective understanding of the social world. While Parsons subordinated individual actors' orientation and action to a normative system, Schutz suggested that social order, i.e., a meaningful world, "is constituted, maintained, and altered through action of actors and only through the action of actors" (Garfinkel 1952: 149). Yet by focusing on intersubjectivity and shared knowledge, Schutz overemphasized actors' efforts to produce a world in common, requiring them to "suspend their differences of perspective and interest" (Heritage 1984: 73). He elaborated on the difficulty of an argument without considering that in the social world, people often ignore and oppose common typifications and agreements.

The analyses by Schutz focused on interpreting the subjective meaning actors ascribe to actions, other people and objects. Garfinkel shifted the focus from the subjective and cognitive to the social and practical accomplishment of social order. Inspired by Schutz's argument that the social order at the center of Parsons' work was an achievement by the actors themselves, he developed a perspective designed to investigate the organization of practical actions in the social world. Nevertheless, "[W]ithin Schutz's theoretical gaze the actors are caught in the frozen postures of actions-in-the-course-of-completion; 'cinema' however is never quite achieved" (Heritage 1984: 73). Garfinkel therefore used Schutz's emphasis of the importance of time for analyzing social action to turn these frozen postures into dynamic meaning-creating processes; in other words, proposing to achieve "cinema."

Garfinkel viewed actions produced in the everyday as accomplished in ways that generate coherent experiences of social situations: "order [...] points only to the characteristics of continuous activity whatever these characteristics may be" (Garfinkel 1952: 149). He deployed Schutz's theoretical framework to investigate the organization of the everyday as experienced by actors in concrete situations. Thereby, Garfinkel interpreted Schutz in a creative way that allowed him to develop his own perspective to explore *social order*.[2] At this stage of the development of his sociology, Garfinkel remained closely aligned to Schutz, while recognizing that a sociological attitude would need to overcome Schutz's suspension of "the possibility of a community between the actor and the observer" (Garfinkel 1952: 112), by understanding participants' or members' relevancies and orientations "in vivo" as he later called it (Garfinkel 2002). In an unpublished manuscript, "[H]e seems here to be acknowledging the achievability of a community of knowledge between actor and observer. Rather than doubting its (possible) existence, he adds (or, rather, says that Schutz adds) an admittedly important question—how is it possible?"(Bilmes 1975: 62). I return to this question when discussing *Ethnomethodology's Program* and the policy of *unique adequacy* in particular.

## Perceiving the Other

His extensive examination of Schutz and Parsons' theories and concepts provided Garfinkel with a basis for the production of *experiments* that he planned to conduct as part of his doctoral research. With these experiments, Garfinkel tried to undermine or "breach" participants' assumption of intersubjectivity and create the *pluralism of worlds* that he had already described in his short story "Color Trouble" when the various participants explained their actions (Hama 2009: 447). The analysis of the experiments required the researcher to use a framework that would allow him to reveal the organization of the participants' experience. Garfinkel drew on Schutz's (1943, 1945b) analysis of the life-world as experienced by actors in the so-called *natural attitude*. Here, Schutz (1945b) had differentiated the natural attitude from attitudes deployed by scientific observers, artists, or when dreaming and had suggested that each of these "provinces of meaning" was characterized by the deployment of a different *cognitive style*.

The cognitive style of the actor in the natural attitude is made up of six characteristics: (a) epoché; (b) form of sociality; (c) mode of attention to life; (d) form of spontaneity; (e) mode of time consciousness; and (f) mode of self-giveness. These dimensions allowed Schutz to analyze how actors orient to the world. Schutz explained the relevance of this organization by applying it, for example, to the province of meaning described as the everyday. Here the actor presents him/herself (a) as wide-awake and acts (b) in the natural attitude; (c) s/he acts within and upon the world, (d) experiences his/her actions as changing the world, (e) acts and communicates within an intersubjective world, and (f) orients to standard time (Garfinkel 1952: 160–161).

Garfinkel took this concept of cognitive style and the six characteristics to describe the natural attitude directly from Schutz's (1945b) essay "On multiple realities." However, he was cautious and said that he "cannot say [...] that the use of which they [the characteristics] are being put or the ways in which I have defined them would be approved by

Dr Schutz" (Garfinkel 1952: 161, Fn.4). For the purpose of his doctoral research, Garfinkel placed his research subjects in a situation where they became doubtful of their ability to judge the character and ability of others and ultimately of themselves (Garfinkel 1952: 391). His interest lay in explaining how the subjects dealt with this doubt (Garfinkel 1952: 403).

As part of his doctoral research project Garfinkel subjected 28 students of medicine to three hour-long experimental interviews. The students were nearly finished with their studies and had begun to prepare themselves to apply for jobs at medical schools. The interviewer (Garfinkel) introduced himself as representative of a medical school who was interested in why applicants experience job interviews as stressful. He began the interviews by first asking them about their concept of a successful applicant: What education and training should they have to be appointed by a medical school? How should they conduct themselves in interviews? After about an hour the interviewer offered the interviewees a chance to listen to a recording of an actual interview. These recorded interviews were fabrications that Garfinkel had created in preparation for the experiments. In the recorded interviews an uneducated, badly behaved applicant used very rough language when answering the interviewer's questions; he smoked during the interview and contradicted the interviewer at various points. At the end he pressurized the interviewer to tell him about his performance in the interview. The replay of the job interview served as a basis for the interviewer to continue the discussion with the student. He invited the student to assess the performance of the applicant in the interview and then informed him/her about the applicant and how her/his performance in the interview was actually assessed.

This information referred to the applicant's family background and character. It strongly contrasted with the interviewee's assessment of the applicant. While the interviewees considered the applicant to be uneducated and uncultivated and unsuitable for a job at a medical school, the interviewer told them that the applicant actually came from a very good family background and had been employed by the medical school. The interviewee experienced the way in which the medical school assessed the applicant and the ways in which s/he had assessed her/him as a contradiction that unsettled them. They responded with inquiries about how other interviewees had assessed the applicant and whether the applicant in fact was successful in the job interview and would now work at the medical school. The interviewer confirmed that the applicant had been accepted for the position at the medical school and was fulfilling all expectations held by the school; furthermore, all the other students had assessed the applicant correctly. Thus, Garfinkel progressively shook the students' belief in their ability to correctly assess the requirements that medical schools bestowed on job applicants. He made the students doubt their ability to assess others and, in light of their plan to soon apply for a job at a medical school themselves, made them worry about their own suitability for such a job. In order to provide the students with an opportunity to correct their assessment of the applicant, the interviewer offered them an opportunity to listen to the recorded interview once more (Garfinkel 1952: 405).

Garfinkel concluded that 25 of the 28 participants in his experiment did not notice they were involved in an experiment. The participants presented themselves as rattled after discovering they had misjudged the applicant. In particular, the interviewees – who were devoted to work as medical doctors – had difficulties dealing with their misjudgment. They responded to the interviewer's statement that they had wrongly assumed the applicant was poorly educated and uncultivated by displaying their astonishment. They used the opportunity to listen to the interview again to correct their original assessment of the applicant and provided accounts for their misjudgment. In many cases, their characterization of the applicant after listening to the job interview for a second time contradicted their original assessment. For example, while originally describing the applicant as "aggressive," after a second listening of the interview the same student described the applicant as "trustworthy." In their responses they attempted to explain their obvious contradictions, for example, by accounting for the applicant's conduct in the interview. They did not characterize the applicant as uneducated and uncultivated, but as a calm and thoughtful person who acted naturally. In providing these accounts, the students literally took the perspective of the applicant and removed the incongruity that had arisen after listening to the interview for the first time (Garfinkel 1952: 495).

By experiencing their assessment of the applicant as misjudgment, the students doubted not only their ability to assess others correctly, but also questioned their sense of being able to assess their own abilities. In his analysis of the experiment, Garfinkel (1952) characterized the job interview as a *province of meaning* where the participants deployed particular communication strategies. These strategies were used to build an acceptable self-image when it was impossible to correct mistakes and misjudgments produced previously. The accounts produced to explain the situation and to revise previous judgments of people were deployed not only to correct the perception of the other, but also to restore the coherence of the participant's attitude to the situation. Thus, the participants were able to remove discrepancies that had arisen in the situation. In other words, the cognitive style participants deployed in the experiments shaped their orientation and attitude in the situation. It was embodied within the interviewees' inquiries and the accounts they gave for their (mis) judgments. In this sense, cognitive style can be compared to Jerome Bruner's discussion of "narrative framing of the world that shapes cognition, what a person actually perceives and how he or she reasons about it" (Garfinkel 2012; Rawls 2013: 310).

From the experiments Garfinkel learned that participants in social situations are concerned with maintaining the social order of the world, even when they have to modify and adapt their perception of the other. He examined the interviewees' responses to the situation they were confronted with in the experiments to explain some of the methods that participants used to restore their sense of order. For example, he found that the students redefined the applicant's situation by aligning their original assessment of the applicant with the interviewer's explanation of their suitability for the job, and they corrected their original assessment of the applicant and acknowledged that they had obviously misjudged them (Garfinkel 1952).

## Tutorial Exercises: *Breaching Experiments*

Garfinkel's doctoral dissertation marked the beginning of an empirical program of research that he continued to pursue over the coming decades and that today we know as *ethnomethodology*. Like his doctoral research, the further development of ethnomethodology relied on theoretical analyses that Garfinkel had already conducted in the 1940s, which, however, were only published recently in *Seeing Sociologically* (Garfinkel 2006 [1948]). At the center of the research program was the use of analytic and empirical research methods that helped to reveal the organization of the everyday and to demonstrate that actors accomplish this organization through practical actions and experience it in concrete situations. His famous "trust" paper (1963) is a pertinent article that elaborates on the relationship between action and experience that he had in mind. The paper explores the relationship between participation in a game such as "tic-tac-toe" (Figure 4.1) and the formal rules that are the basis for the game, in order to shed light on the methodical production of the everyday.

**Figure 4.1**   Tic-Tac-Toe

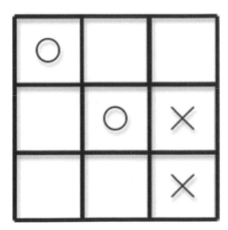

Schutz (1945b) described games as a "province of meaning," such as the worlds of dreams and science. They differ from other provinces of meaning by a particular "tension of consciousness": "epoché," i.e., attitude to the world; a particular form of spontaneity; "a specific form of sociality"; "a specific form of self-experience"; and "a special time perspective." The rules of games or *basic rules,*[3] as Garfinkel (1963) called them at this point in the development of his sociology, provide participants with a scheme they can orient to when producing their actions. Thus, each of their actions becomes intelligible for others as contributing to the game (1963: 190). The basic rules turn every move in the game into an "observable-and-reportable,"[4] i.e., an *accountable* event, as Garfinkel (1967c: 1) called it later; all actors participating in the game in one way or other can use the rule book to decide whether an action is accomplished according to the rules that make up the normative order of the game (1963: 194). The rule book of tic-tac-toe states that the two players can make moves on nine given fields; moves are made one player at a time until one of them has been able to place three of her/his symbols in a row. The availability of such basic rules allows all players to:

- have expectations regarding the procedure of the game;

- have the expectation that all of them have the same opportunities for action in the game; and

- expect that all of them base their actions on the assumption that all players have expectations with regard to each other's actions and to the procedure of the game.

The playing of the game requires the participants to be committed to these rules. They know the rules of the game and perform actions according to them. Or, if they act in violation of the rules, the rule book is used as a resource to sanction the actor and account for the sanctioning by describing the action as deviant. This focus on games and rule books, however, was rather limiting and Garfinkel expanded his notion of trust beyond a mere normative order to the order of the everyday. He suggested that parties in a given situation mutually assume that

Figure 4.2

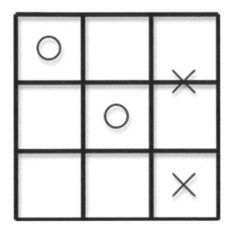

they orient to the events and objects around them in the same way and use the same methods to make sense of them. Actions in a situation are seen as reciprocally accountable because participants maintain a given orientation to a situation and take for granted that others maintain their orientation as well (cf. Watson 2009). In some of the breaching experiments he asked his students to systematically break rules when playing games such as tic-tac-toe. For example, he asked them to rub out crosses their partners had made in fields and place their own in more favorable positions or to place their symbols not in the field but on the lines (Figure 4.2). On return to class the students reported their friends' reactions to their rule breaking.

The analysis of the observations of rule breaking in games that his students reported on their return to class revealed the existence of "non-contractual elements of the contract," as Durkheim famously called them, or "the unstated and *essentially* unstatable terms that the contracting parties took for granted as binding upon their transactions" (Garfinkel 1967g: 173). By breaking the constitutive expectations implied in games and their rule books, the anomic properties of events during games are multiplied. The impact this has for the organization of games varies, depending on the extent to which basic rules are intentionally followed and occur independently from the individual properties of the players. Deviations from the basic rules, such as the erasing of moves or the placing of symbols on the lines between fields, encourage attempts to "normalize" the discrepancy between the normative and practical order, as the co-players attempt to find an explanation for each other's actions. Garfinkel remarked that in such situations participants' orientation to the situation of the game is shaken and the "thinking-as-usual" (Eberle 1984) is questioned and put into doubt. The individual is momentarily in crisis as s/he doubts the organized procedure of situations and loses *trust* in the expected organization of events.

While, early on, Garfinkel focused his tutorials on games and rules in games[5], in the trust paper (1963: 206–209) he made clear that games fundamentally differ from the everyday. He described games as an "artificial world in a microcosm" (1963: 207) that have a "peculiar time structure": the duration of the game is played and the time in which the rules of the game remain valid are clearly defined. "To be 'in the game' involves by definition the suspension of the presuppositions and procedures of 'serious' life" (ibid.) and to align with the "basic rules" (ibid.) that in effect are "objective rules" (ibid.) as long as the game is being played. Recognizing the differences between games and the everyday, Garfinkel soon designed tutorials that were conducted in natural social situations.

Garfinkel (1967e [1962]) examined some of these experiments in his article "Common-sense Knowledge of Social Structures: The Documentary Method of Interpretation in Lay and Professional Fact Finding," published in *Studies*. Garfinkel used these tutorials that had games at their center to reveal the relationship of basic rules and background expectancies that underpin the social order of the everyday.[6] Games are organized by norms that regulate participants' conduct. These norms are drawn on to account for descriptions of actions as deviant and sanctionable. In other words, participants can rely on these norms and *trust* in their existence as invariant characteristics of situations. When producing their actions, participants can assume that the social world is organized as they expect it and that others will act in ways that can be expected within the given situation.

Formal-analytic sociology often relies on a concept of social order that is maintained by norms. Garfinkel, however, used his tutorials to systematically argue against this model of social order. From his analysis of Schutz he had learned that the actor is not a norm-guided player in a game or a "judgmental dope" or "cultural dope" (Garfinkel 1967d [1964]: 67), as he ironically characterized the way in which the actor is portrayed in formal sociology.[7] His doctoral research, as well as his tutorial exercises, added to this understanding by demonstrating that social order does not collapse in light of violations of norms, as long as participants remain able to make sense of the situation: "Therefore he explained social order not by normative but by constitutive rules and by sense-making" (Eberle 2012: 141).

To put it another way, Garfinkel now considered social order as continuously produced through actions that render it "observable-and-reportable" without revealing the trust that underpins it. Trust "is a presumptive phenomenon and therefore tacitly attended to by members" (Watson 2009: 477). Garfinkel's breaching experiments[8] or tutorials in everyday settings generated situations where participants encountered unexpected events that installed confusion or frustration; their *trust* in the orderliness of the situation, i.e., in the presumed alignment of orientations, was shattered. In response to these events, the participants made jokes or tried to explain them to normalize the situation. One well-known tutorial in this regard was the task that asked students to challenge the taken-for-granted assumptions about relationships the students had with their parents. Garfinkel suggested, for example, that they pretended to be lodgers in their parents' home rather than family members. By "violating" the taken-for-grantedness of their status in the home they confused their parents who then attempted to normalize the situation by providing accounts for the actions that did not fit in.

The program of research that Garfinkel proposed became designed to explore how sense-making is not a cognitive and subjective process, but rather an intersubjective and observable practice. He therefore suggested conducting studies which investigated the invariant properties of everyday situations that allow participants to act in a competent manner and through which they make observable and reportable the organization of situations, such as a sales interaction, a conversation among family members, a traffic jam, or a waiting queue. The rules and background expectancies are "the socially standardized and standardizing, 'seen but unnoticed', expected, background features of everyday scenes" (Garfinkel 1967d: 36). Participants use these background expectancies to design their actions in situations and to make sense of situations. Thus, events they encounter become intelligible as "appearances-of-familiar-events" (ibid.). For participants, the organization of the everyday is unproblematic; there is no need for a formalized rule book or a social scientific description of the social order based on an analytic scheme or system of categories. Instead, everyday life is always already orderly and familiar to the participants and therefore in their day-to-day lives participants do not make explicit background expectancies; they only orient to them and bestow them with relevance in situations of breakdown and crisis. When participants encounter such crises, they respond to them by "post-hoc" accounts that explain the circumstances of their emergence. Garfinkel found that while such post-hoc explanations and descriptions of situations only incompletely represent the meaning of action, they tend to be specific enough to allow the actors to continue to participate in the situation.

In Garfinkel's view, the meaning of action arises from the specific circumstances of their production. Participants treat each action as "documenting" the social structure that, within the situation, is tacitly implied in people's actions. Garfinkel derived this usage of the term *document* from an article by Karl Mannheim (1952) in which he developed the "documentary method of interpretation." He (1967d [1964]: 40) used Mannheim's "documentary method" to explain that the pattern underlying action "was not only derived from a course of individual documentary evidences but the documentary evidences in their turn were interpreted on the basis of 'what was known' and anticipatorily knowable about the underlying patterns." Thus, he points to the reflexive relationship between the meaning of action and the context of its production. Through the formulation of this argument, Garfinkel again deliberately "mis-read" a sociological classic and linked Mannheim's "documentary method" to Schutz's concept of types by aiming to develop a method through which people remain able to act in contingent situations.

In a paper in which Garfinkel elaborates on the use of sociological concepts for psychiatrists he (1956b) links the "documentary method of interpretation" to the concept of "understanding" that in those years was discussed in the context of the emerging interpretive approaches to sociology. Garfinkel (1956b: 193) explains that rather than being a method that sociologists (and psychiatrists) could use to "understand" people's action, it was a method that people in their daily lives would ordinarily deploy to make sense of others' action. "It involves the treatment of a sign's referent as 'the document of...' as 'pointing to' an underlying pattern. Not only is the underlying pattern derived from its individual documentary evidence, but the individual documentary evidences are in their turn interpreted on the basis of 'what we know' about the underlying pattern."

Although Garfinkel continued to use tutorial exercises in the years following the trust paper, he focused on the analysis of "familiar scenes," such as interactions in everyday situations whose organization is doubted when he or his students deployed "troublemakers" who generated unexpected events and incongruity or "pluralism of worlds," as he (1952: 97) called it in his doctoral dissertation. These demonstrations helped Garfinkel to investigate actors' knowledge and understanding of social structures (Garfinkel 1967d [1964]). In Herbert Spiegelberg's (1981 [1960]) words, the tutorial exercises served Garfinkel as "aids to a sluggish imagination" (1967d [1964]: 38).

Beginning with his doctoral research project and the theoretical analysis he developed in the 1940s, Garfinkel developed an original *sociological attitude* that is known today as *ethnomethodology*. By ethnomethodology, Garfinkel was not describing a particular sociological method but a particular orientation, attitude, or, as he termed it in *Seeing Sociologically* (2006), a particular *cognitive style* that, when adopted, allowed the sociologist to make sense of social order as continuously produced and experienced by the actor. In this sense, as we will see in the following chapters more clearly, Garfinkel's ethnomethodology respecified the question of method and knowledge in studies of the social. It gave preference to the capacities of individuals (members) to draw upon their own knowledge of social order over the propriety of knowledge gained through quasi-empirical or quasi-scientific means. From this perspective, *methodology* in the sociological sense serves only as a technique for obtaining data that explicate how some form of the social is created by participants in concrete situations. For Garfinkel, it was unimportant how these data came into existence (i.e., quantitative or qualitative methods), as he noted that "*any* data gathering technique leaves a bread-crumb trail to *the social* it seeks to describe" (Patrick Watson, Personal Communication). In the following chapter I further explore the development of Garfinkel's sociological attitude and perspective in order to find out "what is ethnomethodology?"

*Chapter 5*

# What Is Ethnomethodology?

By adopting a focus on everyday practices and the ongoing production of social reality, ethnomethodology positions itself in contrast to theory and research in "traditional" or "conventional" sociology (Garfinkel 2002). When the *Studies* were published and ethnomethodology became almost fashionable, contemporary sociologists were surprised, if not stunned. They considered Garfinkel's project to be irrelevant and without contribution to the important questions society was grappling with in the 1960s and 1970s; it was the time of the Cold War, the Cuban Missile Crisis, the Civil Rights Movement and Martin Luther King, the assassination of JFK, the Vietnam War, and the student revolt, among others. In his opening speech to the 1974 ASA Conference, Lewis Coser (1975) described ethnomethodologists as a splinter group and compares them to a sect without interest in and relevance for sociological debates. He likened Garfinkel to a leader of a sect with the ethnomethodologists as his following. His remarks were also reflected in the British-Czech philosopher and anthropologist Ernest Gellner's (1975) response to ethnomethodology, calling it the "Californian Way of Subjectivity."

Ever since ethnomethodology arrived on the sociological scene, questions have been asked concerning its relationship to sociology. Is it a novel sociological perspective or, in fact, an academic discipline in its own right (Goldthorpe 1973)? At a conference known as the "Purdue Symposium on Ethnomethodology" (Hill and Crittenden 1968), Garfinkel responded evasively to the question of whether he saw himself as a sociologist. His colleague Edward Rose, however, was clear and open in his assessment "that ethnomethodology constitutes a deep and strong critique of sociology," because sociologists were developing a theory about the social world before they began with their analysis (Rose in Hill and Crittenden 1968).

This chapter discusses Garfinkel's development of the ethnomethodological program after having completed his doctoral dissertation. At the center of this chapter is the question, "what is ethnomethodology?" By explicating the key principles of the ethnomethodological program, the chapter also begins to show how Garfinkel grounded ethnomethodology within, and related it to rather than separating it from, sociology.

## The Elevator Question

It has happened to many of us sociologists. We enter an elevator or have a cup of coffee when an acquaintance asks, "What is sociology?" We are then often unable to immediately come up with a suitable response, mumble a textbook definition, and leave the situation dissatisfied. Garfinkel reported that at ASA conferences he regularly encountered similar situations and was often asked, "What is ethnomethodology?" He also found it difficult to provide a satisfying response and continued to work on the development of an appropriate answer to the "elevator question" up to the end of his working life. In various articles and books he addressed the question and expanded on what the ethnomethodological program of research was and what one could learn by doing ethnomethodology.

Garfinkel offered a first answer to the question "what is ethnomethodology?" in an article based on a presentation[1] he and Saul Mendlovitz delivered at the 1954 ASA Conference. In the article, Garfinkel and Mendlovitz drew on their analysis of the work of jurors in a court in Wichita. Their analysis was concerned with the deliberations of jurors that Fred Strodtbeck, a friend and colleague of Garfinkel, had audio-recorded as part of the Jury Project. They augmented their inspection of the audio-recordings with an analysis of interviews and investigated what work was involved in jury deliberations.

When Garfinkel and Mendlovitz began their analysis of the data, they planned to use *interaction process analysis*, a research method that Robert Freed Bales (1976 [1950]) had developed in Harvard. This method provided the researcher with a coding system that s/he could use to analyze the processes of action among members of small groups. Garfinkel, however, had some doubts that this method would deliver on their research purpose, i.e., to find out how participants were organizing their action in jury deliberations. Garfinkel and Mendlovitz then discussed possible research methods with Edward Shils (1911–1995), the well-known sociologist from Chicago, who had a leading role in the Jury Project. He advised the two young researchers against using interaction process analysis, and they therefore decided to develop their own method of analysis. In later publications, Garfinkel described the process that led them to a decision about the research method as the following:

> When Strodtbeck proposed to a law school faculty to administer Bales' Interaction Process Analysis categories, Shils complained: 'By using Bales [sic] Interaction Process Analysis I'm sure we'll learn what about a jury's deliberations makes them a small group. But we want to know what about their deliberations makes them a jury' (Garfinkel, Lynch, and Livingston 1981: 133).

Mendlovitz and Garfinkel thereupon turned to their audio-recordings and developed their own method to analyze them. They were particularly interested in the analysis of the knowledge and methods that the participants in jury deliberations deployed to render their meetings intelligible as those of a jury and not of some other kind of small group or organization. The term *organization* that Garfinkel used in his analyses fundamentally differed from that of an organization as "a concrete structure" found in the world like 'chairs' or 'tables' (Garfinkel 1956b). Rather, at this stage of his intellectual development, Garfinkel's interest lay with "features of organized social life" (1956b: 183), an interest that he had arrived at through intensive examination of Parsons' (1951) *The Social System*. Parsons' concept of *organization:*

> Parsons' "organization places particular stress on the person's perceived situation as a set of mutually anticipated, expected, recollect-

ed events ... A person is a chauffeur thereby, not only on the basis of the service he expects to render the rider, but on the basis of the treatment that he gets in return (Garfinkel 1956b: 182–183).

Since the 1960s this consideration of 'organization' as an "organization of activities" (Garfinkel 1956b: 183) became one of the principal areas of concern for Garfinkel and other ethnomethodologists (Bittner 1965). Their studies were concerned with the "techniques" and "methods" through which organization is accomplished and becomes observable and intelligible. Garfinkel introduced the term *ethnomethods* to describe these techniques and methods of making social organization "observable-and-reportable," i.e., *accountable* (Garfinkel 1967c: 1). In so doing, he drew on the ethno-sciences, such as "ethno-musicology," for the syllable "ethno-" to mark that these methods are used by a community with shared knowledge and language. The discipline that analyzed these methods he called *ethnomethodology.*

Garfinkel together with his students and colleagues gradually turned ethnomethodology into a distinctive independent area of research. Although over the years various publications (Garfinkel 1972, 1974; Livingston 1987; Mehan and Wood 1975; Turner 1974) have explained what ethnomethodology is, Garfinkel was regularly confronted with the "elevator question." Unfortunately some of the responses that ethnomethodologists gave were perceived as arrogant and ignorant of sociology; Goldthorpe , for example, suggested that:

> the typical reaction of more 'conventional' sociologists to these new movements of thoughts could perhaps be best described as one of somewhat bewildered doubt, and such hostility as was displayed was probably aroused more by the manner of their presentation than by their actual content." (Goldthorpe, 1973: 449)

Thus, a distance between ethnomethodology and sociology was created that has debilitated the impact of ethnomethodology on theoretical, methodological, and empirical debates to the present day. In the 1960s and 1970s established social scientists considered ethnomethodology as "anti-sociology," their analyses as vacuous, and their concerns of study as irrelevant for sociology. The aforementioned "Purdue Symposium on Ethnomethodology," organized by Richard Hill and Kathleen Stones Crittenden (1968), was an attempt to facilitate discussion between ethnomethodologists and sociologists and to help ameliorate the rejection that ethnomethodology faced at conferences and gatherings of sociologists. The symposium offered Garfinkel and his colleagues, including Aaron Cicourel, Edward Rose, Harvey Sacks, and David Sudnow, an opportunity to explain their position and discuss their perspective with established sociologists like Howard Becker, Lindsey Churchill, and Kathleen Stones Crittenden.

At the symposium, Garfinkel was offered the opportunity to explicate his perspective and purpose in developing ethnomethodology. He began his explanation by describing the origin of the term and referring to the Jury Project that had sharpened his concern for the production of organization. He said that at some point, he and Mendlovitz had begun to put together their "ideas about how the jurors knew what they were doing in doing" (Garfinkel in Hill and Crittenden 1968: 5). Their question was, "what makes them jurors?" (Garfinkel in Hill and Crittenden 1968: 6), which encouraged them to further ask what knowledge about legal procedures and processes the jurors brought to bear in their work that made them recognizable as "jurors". They had observed that jurors used different techniques from, for example, scientists when looking for truth. The jurors' concern was with the adequacy of accounts and descriptions that they produced as part of their deliberations (ibid.). During the deliberations, the jurors reflected on the status of their decisions, were they legal, just, and fair? When jurors accounted for their decisions, they would point out that, as jurors, they could legitimately make certain statements in light of the evidence presented in a given case. In other words, Garfinkel and Mendlovitz's analysis demonstrated that jurors become jurors by deploying a particular "methodology" that made their work intelligible as the work of jurors.

These studies of jurors had great influence on future ethnomethodological studies of situations and events, or "familiar scenes" as

Garfinkel (1967d [1964]) called them in his *Studies*. Familiar scenes are identifiable as particular social occasions because they are practically and intelligibly organized in recognizable ways, rather than dependent on the presence of particular people. Ethnomethodologists can learn about jury deliberations by exploring, e.g., the social, demographic, and educational backgrounds of participants. However, the procedures and processes through which the deliberations are conducted do not rely on particular people being present. Individual jurors are replaceable at any point in time and people who arrive in a room where a deliberation takes place quickly recognize it as such an event and immediately know how to participate in it. Those properties that Garfinkel (2002) described as "autochthonous order properties" are the same for juror deliberations and other organizations, such as waiting queues and traffic jams, dance events, workplaces, and others. Waiting queues are not organized by specific individual people; the people standing in a queue (or the individual dancers and workers) are interchangeable without the queue disappearing as an observable phenomenon. Instead, organizations are practically achieved by their members, who bring about the phenomenon of the queuing, the dancing, the working by virtue of producing their actions in specific ways. It is the production and design of these actions that makes them intelligible as actions of a particular kind of organization. Thus, the phenomenon of the queuing, dancing, working, etc. acquires its properties and is produced as long as 'waiting queue actions', 'dancing actions', 'working actions' are produced. The phenomenon disappears when members engage in different kinds of action, for example, when they turn the queue into a huddle around the entrance of the arriving bus, or leave the dance floor and go to the bar (Garfinkel and Livingston 2003).

In a different investigation, Garfinkel (1997) explored the work of staff at a Suicide Prevention Center (SPC) in Los Angeles. The members of the SPC who participated in his study were in charge of explaining how a person "really" died. To address this question the SPC staff gathered and inspected all the material they could find near the dead body, including the body of the deceased, written documents, and objects like instruments and vessels, as well as stories and rumors about the dead person that they heard from neighbors, acquaintances, and relatives of the deceased. After the investigation, the SPC staff produced a report containing a relatively small amount of specific details about the circumstances of the person's death. It was entirely possible that after publication of the report, concerns would be raised that some of the findings were inaccurate or that some of the procedures used by the SPC staff were against the rules. "The prevailing feature of the inquiry is that nothing about it remains assured except the organized occasions of its uses" (Garfinkel 1967c: 15). The features of such reports, however, were not unexpected. Indeed, it was assumed that investigations into the death of a person remained incomplete. It was seen as an obvious property of such reports that they did not cover all the details that were possibly related to the death and that further examinations and improvements on the report were always possible. Yet, despite these short-comings and the incompleteness of the reports, it was recognized that the findings reported in them were important and correct, and helped to move the work of the SPC staff forward.

The incompleteness and weaknesses of the reports were rarely subjected to discussion and debate. If asked for further information, the SPC staff would explain the rationality of their work. They produced *accounts* of actions that had led to the description or *account* of the circumstances of the person's death. These accounts revealed that the explanations given in a report for the death of the person were "indexical" in character. The rationality of the explanations was based on the situation in which they were produced. Subsequent explanations that became necessary when reported findings were questioned or put in doubt arose in different circumstances altogether and therefore were grounded in a different rationality.

When Garfinkel described the work of the SPC staff and jurors as "methodology," this was fundamentally different from what sociologists had conventionally considered methodology. In sociology, a *methodology* provides the theoretical frame for the use of particular methods; methodology here is comparable to a rule book that frames the deployment of methods. Garfinkel, however, in his explanation, relied on Felix Kaufmann's (1944) use of the term *methodology*. Kaufmann conceived of "methodology" as a rule book that did not structure events but that participants produced only in the process of using it (Garfinkel 1967c: 6, Fn.5 ). In Garfinkel's view, rules were not instructions that people followed, rather, rules were properties of situations people act in (Garfinkel 1967f: 106). Participants know what a situation is because it is accomplished in and through their actions and those of other participants. When participants encounter a situation, they design their actions to make them fit and align with the continuously produced context and to contribute to its production. A game like basketball, for example, becomes intelligible as such not because a rule book defines the players' actions, but because the players design their actions in ways that turn the situation into a game of basketball. If situations arise that put the basketball game into doubt, referees draw on the rule book to account for their decision to intervene in the ongoing proceedings of the game; the rules are a resource the referees can use to legitimize their intervention and to restore the order of the game (Askins, Carter, and Wood 1981; Macbeth 2012). In practice, however, referees are rarely asked to legitimize decisions, but sports analysts often refer to the "rules" or the "rule book" in their commentaries on referees' decisions.

With his explanation of the relationship between rules and social order, Garfinkel (1963; Garfinkel and Sacks 1970; Heritage 1984) critiqued theories, concepts, and models that had been generated to explain human action in its entirety. He drew on Wittgenstein's (1973 [1951]) *Philosophical Investigations*, where the philosopher argued that rules and instructions were insufficient to describe situations. In this view, rules and instructions are abstract and therefore incomplete descriptions of actions because they ignore the contingent circumstances in which specific actions are undertaken. Rules and instructions are deployed repeatedly and each time is another 'first time' because the circumstances of their use change. In addition, they cannot be repaired by analyses of the formal properties of language and practical reasoning (Garfinkel 1963; Garfinkel and Sacks 1970; Heritage 1984).

In other words: rules and descriptions always leave an undefined space. The practices implied here might be called *unspecifying* practices and Garfinkel (1967c: 20–21) differentiated four such *ad hoc considerations*: "et cetera," "unless," "let it pass," and "factum valet" ["i.e., an action that is otherwise prohibited by a rule, is counted correct once it is done" (Garfinkel 1967c: 21)]. He considered them to be "commonsense practices" that people ordinarily deploy when accounting for their actions. For example, Garfinkel studied the work involved in coding information about applicants to an outpatient clinic in order to make decisions about their treatment (Garfinkel, 1967h). The coders regularly compared their codes, prompting Garfinkel's interest in the process of how the co-workers checked and assessed the reliability of the codes. He found that the coders deployed a practice of "ad hoc-ing" (Garfinkel 1967c) that allowed them to deal with inconsistencies and uncertainty. They "used the same *ad hoc* considerations in order to recognize the relevance of the coding instructions to the organized activities of the clinic" (Garfinkel 1967c: 21). For example, the practices of the *et cetera* were unavoidably implied in every rule book: "[Y]ou find in the complex of ordinary, mundane accounts that there are practices for locating monsters but there are also practices for burying them. There are practices for refusing the existence of exceptions" (Garfinkel in Hill and Crittenden 1968: 213).

In a similar way, the other ad hoc considerations were examined for their relevance for the coders' work. Garfinkel (1967c: 21–23) demonstrated that "*ad hoc* considerations are a critical features of coding procedures" although coders would strive "to minimize or even eliminate the occasions" in which they were deployed. These considerations were used by coders in order to specify the coding instructions and "operate as the grounds for and as methods to advance and secure researchers' claims to have coded in accordance with 'necessary and sufficient' criteria" (ibid).

Coders obviously had an interest in the close relationship between the content of the clinical records and the reality of activities in the clinic, "the social-order-in-and-of-clinic activities" (Garfinkel 1967c:

23). The coder, therefore, "must know the order of the clinic's activities" to relate them to their representations in the records. Thus, the clinical records were treated by the coders "as an appearance-of-the-order" of the activities in the clinic (Garfinkel 1967c: 23). Once this relationship between records and reality was clear, the coder could use the ad hoc considerations to make sense of content in the records in light of her/his knowledge of the reality in the clinic.

In the beginning of this chapter I mentioned Garfinkel's difficulties in responding to other sociologists' question "what is ethnomethodology?" In *Studies* (1967a) Garfinkel devoted an entire chapter to this question. This response, however, was not the end, but only the beginning of the development of the ethnomethodological program that Garfinkel elaborated on over the course of his entire career.

# Chapter 6

# Ethnomethodology's Program

When Garfinkel began to develop the ethnomethodological program, he positioned it in relationship to an already existing large body of sociological research produced over the course of at least 100 years (Garfinkel 1967a). Talcott Parsons, Edward Shils, and Alfred Schutz, who all contributed markedly to Garfinkel's academic career, now are considered to be sociological classics. They themselves were influenced by Max Weber and Emile Durkheim's work; Parsons in fact translated some of Weber's books into English.

As the subtitle (*Working Out Durkheim's Aphorism*) of Garfinkel's (2002) *Ethnomethodological Program* revealed, he had a particular interest in addressing some of Durkheim's concerns and the notion of *social facts*, i.e., laws, currencies, language, institutions, and habits (Durkheim 1982 [1895]). In the main, sociological textbooks have interpreted Durkheim's rule to "study social facts as 'things'" literally. They consider social facts as, "aspects of social life that shape our actions as individuals, such as the state of the economy or the influence of religion. [...] social facts are ways of acting, thinking or feeling that are external to individuals and have a reality of their own" (Giddens 2009: 13). In this view, social facts are theoretical constructs that exist independently from and impact on individuals and their actions.

Garfinkel aims to develop a program of research that puts a different spin on the contemporary understanding of Durkheim's concept of social facts. In the preface to the *Studies,* Garfinkel (1967b) wrote:

> [I]n contrast to certain versions of Durkheim that teach that the objective reality of social facts is sociology's fundamental principle, the lesson is taken instead, and used as a study policy, that the objective reality of social facts *as* an ongoing accomplishment of the concerted

activities of daily life, with the ordinary, artful ways of that accomplishment being by members known, used, and taken for granted, is, for members doing sociology, a fundamental phenomenon (Garfinkel 1967b: vii).

Here, Garfinkel read Durkheim differently from the way he conventionally is interpreted in sociology and took the position that social facts are concrete things, not theoretical concepts: "The concreteness of things necessarily depends on, and are produced in and through, complex mutually recognizable social practices enacted by participants in social scenes" (Rawls 2002: 2).Garfinkel developed his ethnomethodological program by focusing on these practices and the accomplishment of social facts. By virtue of this practical definition of the accomplishment of social facts, social order, and organization, Garfinkel placed ethnomethodology in opposition to the view of many of his contemporary social scientists. While traditional sociologists started with the assumption that *social order* was a theoretical concept, made visible through sociological and statistical analysis, Garfinkel argued that organization and structure were a fundamental property of the everyday activities that participants ongoingly, observably, and intelligibly produced.

Garfinkel explained the difference between established sociological theories and ethnomethodology in the following way: sociological theory usually begins with the proposition that objective reality is comprised of social facts. Like Parsons, such sociologists assumed that actors in social situations always encounter a preexisting shared culture and align their action with rules and norms if they want to avoid their actions being sanctioned for deviating from the norms. The premise of such sociological theory, therefore, is the presumption that the social world is principally unorganized and only gains *order* when the idea of an existing shared culture and a system of rules is deployed (Garfinkel 1967a, 2002).

When developing his general thesis of the *reciprocity of perspectives,* Schutz (1953) had critiqued this way of defining the organization of the everyday; he argued that the reciprocity of perspectives was not a theoretical construct, but an actual and ongoing achievement. Garfinkel further advanced Schutz's critique of social scientific concepts that presumed society, and therewith all social events and situations, was determined by rules, norms, and values. He pointed to the complexity, dynamics, and contingency of the everyday and argued that social situations were interactional products and achievements. In an ironic and, at times, polemical manner, he described the "man-in-the-sociologist's-society" as a *cultural dope* or *judgmental dope* who generated the stable properties of society by acting and interacting in a previously defined framework of demands and requirements, as well as within a given range of alternative actions (Garfinkel 1967d [1964]) .

This critique was based on the distinction between scientific and everyday rationality that Garfinkel had already developed in *Seeing Sociologically* (Garfinkel 2006 [1948]) and in his doctoral dissertation (1952). By generating a model of the actor and her/his knowledge and orientation to the world, social scientists produced a dummy that had nothing in common with the concrete actor in specific situations. Garfinkel argued that characteristics that scientific observers subscribed to as the imagined standards of their investigative and theorizing conduct were used to construct the model of a person who acts in a manner governed by these ideals (Garfinkel 1967d). Anne Rawls (2008b: 53) explains the short-coming of the model of the rational actor:

> Assuming a rational man [...] results in creating a model of the actor who is a dummy—and whose own experiences count for nothing. It is the observer (or the model) who decides everything in rational man theory. The observer's reason is always complete, while the actor's reason is always incomplete (because the model requires perfect knowledge of the whole model—which only the observer has).

Instead, Garfinkel suggested shifting the focus from an imagined actor to the "constitutive practices" and thus treating the actor as competent and having sufficient information to be able to act in the situation at hand. In Garfinkel's view the actors' competence and knowledge to act in the situation are a precondition for the production of mutually intelligible actions. Rawls (2008b: 53) summarizes Garfinkel's argument:

> The actor must be competent to both produce and recognize practices in order to make any mutually intelligible sense. They must be morally competent as well because they must both trust the competence and commitment of others and be trusted in return: a gift exchange at a highly detailed sophisticated sequential level of interaction.[1]

Garfinkel therefore proposes to study the rational properties of activities that are accessible to analysis and asks, how can ethnomethodology investigate the rationality of the everyday? And how are the outcomes of ethnomethodology's research different from those of "traditional" sociologists?

Garfinkel argued that traditional sociology developed and deployed theories and concepts, as well as "formal-analytic methods," that had nothing in common with the social world. Traditional sociologists were not concerned with exploring the contingent details of the social world, but rather, "they treat order as an aggregate result of individual action in a context of either structurally constrained or goal-oriented activity" (Rawls 2008a: 703). Hence, sociologists relied on statistical research methods to generate order from their scientific perspective, rather than from the perspective of the "members" of society. Garfinkel (1988) described this theoretical and methodological basis of traditional sociology that aggregated and generalized over contingent specifics as "Parsons' Plenum" (Garfinkel 1988). In doing so, he rejected Parsons' view that there was no orderliness in the plenum, "which is a reference to the fullness of contingent detail that resides in mundane experiences" (Maynard 1996: 2). Rather than ascribing orderliness to external stimuli, such as a normative system, or internalized meanings, "the organization of everyday interaction is due to participants' own contingently embodied activities and actions as those arise in and as the concrete plentitude of lived experience" (Maynard 1996: 2).

Garfinkel (1991) expanded this notion of Parsons' plenum by suggesting that Parsons, as "the spokesperson for the social science movement" differentiates between the "concreteness of organizational things on the one hand and real society that methods of constructive analysis could provide on the other" (ibid.: 14). Traditional sociologists such as Parsons proposed that only by using formal-analytic methods were social scientists able to describe *order*. In light of this argument sociologists have conducted myriad studies that now make up a corpus of knowledge and literature that is the intellectual basis for the "worldwide social science movement" (Garfinkel 2002, 2007a; Garfinkel and Wieder 1992).

Garfinkel criticized the basis of the "social science movement" because, in his view, it was based on the distinction between the constructed order and real society. His critique implied that traditional sociology could only construct the order in real society by using formal-analytic methods (Psathas 1999).Traditional sociological analyses ignored "the enacted, unmediated, directly and immediately witnessable details of immortal ordinary society" (Garfinkel 2002: 97) because they relied on commonsense sociological thinking. They generated glosses of the organization of activities, leaving Durkheim's social facts unexplored. Therefore, they were not different from members' mundane constructions of order in the everyday; members, after all, were folk sociologists (Wieder 1974). Zimmerman and Pollner (1970) then argue that in light of the recognition that the domain of sociologists and people in the everyday is the same, some sociologists would ask, "so what," because they as scientists would see themselves as better equipped to grasp social reality than lay people. Their studies are produced to enrich the sociological knowledge of society.

Ethnomethodology aims to move beyond constructing order just for the purpose of adding to the corpus of the worldwide social science movement. As Garfinkel and Wieder (1992) argued, the ethnomethodological perspective on Durkheim's *immortal society* is "asymmetrically alternate" to the perspective offered by traditional sociology. Garfinkel suggested that social order exists independently from the formal-analytic methods that social scientists deploy to study it. And because of their reliance on formal-analytic methods, sociologists are unable to grasp the practices through which social order is produced; these methods do not allow access to the practical organization of these activities. Garfinkel argued that

> [T]he phenomena that escape are empirically the case and empirically researchable. Their escape cannot be imagined. They escape from carefully designed and carefully administered empirically grounded social analytic theory. That they escape and just how they escape are instructably observable and instructably reproducible. Just what escapes and just how they escape are phenomena of immortal ordinary society. Their escape is socially systematic. The phenomena that escape specify Durkheim's immortal, ordinary society (Garfinkel, 2002: 133).

The result is an asymmetric relationship between ethnomethodology and "conventional" sociology. Ethnomethodology examines phenomena of social order that are also of interest to traditional sociologists; traditional sociologists, however, use formal-analytic methods that are not suitable for studying the phenomena of social order that ethnomethodologists discover through their research.

Ethnomethodological analyses use methods and principles that Garfinkel elaborated throughout his career. In his book *Ethnomethodology's Program* (Garfinkel 2002) discussed these methods and principles in some detail. Looking back at Garfinkel's development of the ethnomethodological program since the 1940s, we can see that these methods and principles instantiate the specifically ethnomethodological attitude that Garfinkel began to explicate in *Seeing Sociologically* (Garfinkel 2006 [1948]). In the following, I discuss the key principles of ethnomethodology: indexicality; the documentary method of interpretation; accounts; reflexivity; unique adequacy; endogenous populations; perspicuous settings; ethnomethodological indifference; and Lebenswelt Pair.

## Indexicality and objectivity

Garfinkel derived the concept of *indexicality* from his breaching experiments. The concept refers to the context boundedness of action and is critical for studies in ethnomethodology as well as conversation analysis that have developed in its light since the 1960s. With the development of the concept of indexicality, Garfinkel radicalized the concept of context that, at the time, was being discussed in linguistics.

In the social sciences there is a common convention to differentiate between *indexical* utterances made in everyday life and *objective* utterances or propositions made by scientists. Scientists are concerned with producing objective and generalizable propositions. The everyday, however, is made up of contingent actions and events; the meaning of "objects" changes over time and, indeed, from one moment to the next. For the social scientist the question, therefore, is how can s/he arrive from the contingent and particular to the objective and generalizable. Or in other words, how the social scientist defines the relationship between the everyday and science is constitutive for the outcome of her/his studies.

As we saw above, Parsons followed an approach that was designed to develop a scientific approach to sociology. He argued for the development of a "grand theory" that would provide a framework for an empirical social science. He believed that such a theoretical framework would allow the sociologist to highlight the orderliness of the social world by relating observations to variables pre-specified by the model. Using this model of the social world, the sociologist could investigate how norms and processes of internalization guarantee social order; the contingencies of the everyday, such as indexical actions, would disappear from view, as the social scientist could produce objective descriptions of the social world.

Schutz proposed a different approach to studying the social world. He aimed to overcome the distinction between indexicality and objectivity by considering every utterance and action as indexical and situated in the "here" and "now." In his analyses he argued that for participants themselves, contingencies and indexicality are unproblematic. They are able to generalize the indexical specifics of the everyday by generating and deploying types and typifications. His interest lay in the ways in which norms and social identity are constituted by virtue of typification processes (Schutz 1967b [1932]).

Garfinkel was not satisfied with the answer Schutz had given to the question about the relationship between indexicality and objectivity because, in his view, Schutz's reliance on typifications was insufficient to understand the emergence of intersubjectivity; processes of typification do not help to explain how participants practically act and interact in concrete situations. Although, for example, a greeting is intelligible as a particular type of action, every participant needs to orally and verbally accomplish the greeting in a particular way, in a concrete situation, and many (perhaps an infinite number of) actions can be seen as greetings. Therefore, it is challenging to even imagine how typifications can overcome and reduce the complexity of situations. Garfinkel "radicalized" or "totalized" the indexical character of meaning by arguing that that indexicality was a property of each and every action. In this sense, he abandoned Husserl and Schutz's distinction of objective, subjective, and situated meaning, and conceived of meaning as fundamentally "situated" and indexical (Eberle 1984).

For participants, the indexicality of social situations does not become problematic because practical reasoning and the use of the "documentary method of interpretation" allow them to continuously accomplish moment-by-moment observable and intelligible socially organized situations. Participants are able to understand and produce intelligible action, despite the meaning of action being context bound; i.e., the meaning of action is influenced by the contingent circumstances of action, and meaning and order are therefore "fleeting" phenomena (Bergmann 1985). Garfinkel talks here of "quiddities" (Garfinkel 1988) and later of "haecceties" (Garfinkel 2007a) of action; both terms refer to the uniqueness and "just-thisness" of meaning (Garfinkel 1991), i.e., to the indexicality of social order. Social order exists only in and for the moment when it is accomplished; a moment later, it has already been transformed and reappears in a new form.

In his doctoral dissertation (1952) and later studies, Garfinkel (1963, 1967) demonstrated how participants deal with doubt and emerging crises in social situations by coming up with explanations that restore social order. His breaching experiments showed that members have competencies, i.e., practical knowledge and skills that they bring to bear in concrete situations, in order to understand and intelligibly produce social order. These competencies and the knowledge that members have about the organization of situations normally remain unquestioned. Indeed, members do not show an interest in the details of situations; they are not concerned with the way in which actions are produced: "For members to be 'interested' would consist of their undertaking to make the 'reflexive' character of practical activities observable" (Garfinkel 1967b: 9). There would be a need for them to ongoingly produce accounts for their actions that examine their artful, moment-by-moment accomplishments.

For participants, therefore, indexicality is unproblematic. Social scientists, however, have difficulty in understanding that order can arise from indexicality. In their analyses they aim to develop objective and generalizable explanations that are valid and transcend the analyzed situation.[2] They consider objectivity and generalizability as key properties of scientific propositions that allow them to claim superiority of their knowledge over that of actors in the everyday. Social scientists arrive at objectivity and generalizability when they deploy methods that are accepted in, and intelligible to, the community of social scientists. In their view, the fundamental basis for the legitimacy of scientific claims is that the social scientific community can assess the objectivity and truth of propositions and the correct deployment of methods that have been used to make such claims.

Garfinkel argued that this social scientific striving for objectivity generates a corpus of knowledge that is fundamentally different from the practical knowledge that actors use in the contingent circumstances of everyday life. Social scientists produce explanations that are useful to scientific discourse, but are ignorant of everyday phenomena. The statistical research methods that had dominated the social sciences since the 1950s created measures that were treated as indicators or signs and representations for intentioned results, and were not used to literally describe observations and findings. Thus, they missed the actual phenomena of everyday social order.

## The Documentary Method of Interpretation

Above I have briefly mentioned the "documentary method of interpretation" that participants themselves use to render their actions intelligible to others and to make sense of others' actions. In the *Studies*, Garfinkel defines the method in the following way:

> The method consists of treating an actual appearance as 'the document of,' as 'pointing to,' as 'standing on behalf of' a presupposed underlying pattern. Not only is the underlying pattern derived from its individual documentary evidences, but the individual documentary evidences, in their turn, are interpreted on the basis of 'what is known' about the underlying pattern. Each is used to elaborate the other" (Garfinkel 1967e [1962]: 78).

In his explanation of the documentary method of interpretation, Garfinkel (1956b, 1967e [1962]) referred to Mannheim's (1952) paper "On the Interpretation of 'Weltanschauung.'"[3] In this paper, Mannheim developed a theory of meaning or knowledge that arises as people communicate and interact with each other. This knowledge is atheoretical and remains unexplicated and tacit. It, however, is embodied in or documented by participants' actions that occur within specific circumstances.

With the documentary method of interpretation Garfinkel pointed to the way in which participants deal with the distinction between objective knowledge and the indexicality of action. Action does not appear on a blank canvas, but is produced against a background or context that itself is dynamic and continuously changing. When people observe an action, they see it emerging within and contributing to a context that provides them with the resources to make sense of the action. Because the action changes the context, its meaning is *indexical*, while, at the same time, intelligible, because it relates to the particular circumstances of its occurrence. Situations do not require people to make explicit this relationship between action and context. Participants tacitly assume that all those present in a situation make sense of the circumstances in the same way. They therefore expect that everybody in the situation is able to understand ongoing events and align her/his action with them. Only when such alignment of actions and sense-making practices is not forthcoming are accounts produced that explain what is going on. Yet, in ordinary circumstances, actions themselves are documents and are treated as documents of the organization of the situation.

## Accounts and Accounting

Ethnomethodological studies analyze everyday activities as members' methods for making those same activities visibly-rational-and-reportable-for-all-practical-purposes, i.e., 'accountable,' as organizations of commonplace everyday activities (Garfinkel 1967b: vii).

Although participants rarely question their actions and the order of situations, they are able to explain the rationality of their actions. In this sense, actions are *account-able,* i.e., observable and reportable. It is worthwhile remembering here that before taking up his studies of sociology, Garfinkel undertook education and training to become an accountant and worked in the family business. This experience provided Garfinkel with experiences in entering accounts through which a particular order is created and made visible in a way that it accounts for the monetary flows in and out of a business. Or, in other words, the activities (*accounting*) of the accountant create relationships between individual accounts through which the balance sheet is generated. If an entry into a balance sheet is questioned, then actions can be conducted that explain and account for the entry to restore the order of the balance sheet.

Garfinkel's training and work as an accountant can be seen as one of the starting points for his development of the concepts of *account* and *accounting* (Rawls 2002: 10). Just as an accountant can provide an account for her/his entries in the balance sheet, so participants in situations are able to account for their actions. Garfinkel argued that when accounting for their actions, participants draw on the same stock of knowledge that they bring to bear when producing their actions. *Accounts* are therefore the "communicative effort" (Garfinkel 2006 [1948]) through which participants make observable and reportable what they are doing and how their actions can be seen and interpreted, and make possible and establish, if only momentarily, intersubjectivity. At the same time, Garfinkel's notion of accountability and account involves a normative aspect, as actors are responsible for their actions: "Garfinkel concluded that shared methods of reasoning generate continuously updated implicit understandings of what is happening in social contexts—a 'running index', as it were, of what is happening in a social event" (Heritage 1988: 128). When participants act in a situation, accountability is always in the background as an ordering principle. The 'running index' is created moment-by-moment and, while often taken for granted, is called upon when participants are asked for overt explanations for their actions.

The everyday largely runs smoothly and participants are not often confronted with crises; completely unanticipated events accounts are taken for granted and remain difficult to explore and analyze by social scientists. Garfinkel (1952, 1963, 1967a) therefore devised *tutorial exercises* that shook participants' trust in situations and encouraged them to search for explanations for actions; i.e., actions that normalize the situation in which, for a moment at least, participants have lost the competence and do not have sufficient information to act. The accounts that participants produced were aspects of action that render reportable why particular actions were accomplished in a particular moment and in a particular way, and why and how they were embedded in the ongoing organization of action. Each action, therefore, is principally accountable, i.e., explainable; an explanation can be found as to why it was produced in the way it was produced at a particular moment (cf. Koschmann 2012; Thielmann 2012).

Mark Peyrot (1982) illustrated the characteristics of an account by using the example of a joke that its recipient does not understand. He highlighted the difference between the telling of a joke and the formulation of a joke, i.e., the explanation why something is humorous or funny. Telling a joke and explaining a joke are not only two different activities, but they are also produced to elicit very different responses: a joke is told to make the co-participant laugh; the explanation of the joke, however, is produced as a means to help the co-participant understand why laughing is the appropriate response to the joke. Or, in other words, when laughing in response to something a participant has said, a co-participant confirms the jokiness of the said and thus contributes to the said as being constituted as a joke. If laughter is not forthcoming, the joke is constituted by providing an account for its jokiness that the co-participant (hopefully) responds to, by saying that they now understand why the said is funny; yet laughter, then, is not or not necessarily produced, because accounts of jokes are rarely humorous.

In Garfinkel's (1967a) research are numerous examples that we could draw on to explain the concept of accounts. When earlier discussing ad hoc considerations, I referred to Garfinkel's study of the ways in which the coders of the information dealt with incongruities between the content of clinical records and their knowledge of the organization of activities within the organization. In such cases, the co-workers were able to make sense of the incongruity by deploying ad hoc practices, such as "et cetera," "unless," "let it pass," and "factum valet." These practices allowed the coders to reinstate the orderliness of the records and make them fit with reality for all practical purposes.

Introductory texts to ethnomethodology often link Garfinkel's analysis of accounts and accounting with the *documentary method of interpretation*. These explanations of accounts and accounting demonstrate the importance of the concept within ethnomethodology because they characterize *accounting practices* as a resource that participants deploy to display and assure themselves that they act in an intersubjective world.

## Reflexivity

*Reflexivity* is at the heart of the tension between ethnomethodology and traditional or "formal-analytic" sociology. Traditional sociology turns members' accounts of social relationships into variables by coding and measuring them. The resulting sociological accounts of social relationships, as published in journal articles and books, are subject to questions regarding their validity and reliability. Sociological theory, therefore, is concerned with questions about the "correct" representation of social order by these accounts. In this sense, sociological theory considers scientific accounts of the social world as superior to the perspective of the everyday actor, because social scientists use theories of knowledge, power, and agency to reflect on action: "reflexivity *in general* offers no guarantee of insight and revelation" (Lynch 2000a: 47). As Wilson and Zimmerman (1979: 54) noted, what sociological theorists "overlook [is] the fact that the production of accounts is a social phenomenon in its own right, including the production of those accounts that are the basis for sociologists' depictions of the social organization of society." In other words, sociological theory ignores the contextual embeddedness of accounts, i.e., it considers accounts of social relationships, such as demographic information, educational background, etc. as stable reference points, without recognizing that these accounts themselves are produced within and are constitutive of, a specific context.

For Garfinkel, the production of accounts itself was embedded within specific circumstances. Such circumstances arise in, and through, the production of actions that gain their sense and significance within the specific circumstances. Hence, Garfinkel not only argued that the meaning of actions was *indexical* (see above), but also that the context within which actions are produced was itself indexical. Despite the contingency of meaning resulting from this indexicality, participants experience the social world as coherent and meaningful. In fact, they hold each other to account for their actions.

In drawing on Gurwitsch's (2012 [1964]) *Field of Consciousness*[4] and Wittgenstein's (1973 [1951]) *Philosophical Investigations* Garfinkel suggested that we are unable to see "the whole as assembled out of pre-existing parts, nor of the parts as determined by some pre-existing whole" (Wilson and Zimmerman 1979: 59). Heritage (1984) referred to optical illusions, such as the well known face/goblet and the rabbit/ duck images. Participants encountering one of these images see either a face or a goblet (rabbit or duck), and what they see depends on their knowledge of the underlying pattern (Heritage 1984: 86). For example, by seeing Figure 5.1 as a duck, participants interpret the left part of the image as beak and the small indention on the right as irrelevant.

When, however, interpreting the same image as a rabbit, the indention gains relevance and is interpreted as the rabbit's mouth, while the left part is seen as the rabbit's ears. In other words, in seeing the image as a duck or a rabbit, people bring to bear their knowledge of animals, and this knowledge overrides the visual cues given by the image (Heritage 1984: 87–88).

In social situations, when people are confronted with indexical expressions, be they oral, visible, or of another kind, they are able to make sense of them by using contextual cues to explain why an action has

Figure 5.1

been produced in a particular moment in a particular way. They contextualize actions and constitute their meaning by relating them to the particular circumstances in which they are produced. Ordinarily, this process of meaning making is "seen but unnoticed." Garfinkel's demonstrations, as well as optical illusions, are a technique in which accounts can be engendered that render participants' background knowledge observable. In social situations, participants ordinarily tacitly assume a common understanding of the world they act in and expect that each other is able to and will understand, indexical expressions:

> The anticipation that persons *will* understand, the occasionality of expressions, the specific vagueness of references, the retrospective-prospective sense of a present occurrence, waiting for something later in order to see what was meant before, are sanctioned properties of common discourse (Garfinkel 1967e [1962]: 87).

In this sense, then, we see that for Garfinkel and ethnomethodology, part and whole, constitute each other; are not independent from each other, but they are reflexively interrelated. Moment-by-moment, participants produce recognizable relationships between actions and the context in which they are produced.

Garfinkel's (1967f) analysis of jury deliberations are a pertinent example to explain the ethnomethodological principle of reflexivity. In their deliberations, jurors discuss arguments, propositions, and statements that prosecutors and lawyers have made in court. They examine the statements and other materials featured in the court proceedings and try to make sense of the events in court. In this sense, the jurors' actions and the statements and events in court are in a *reflexive* relationship to the deliberations. The meetings become intelligible as deliberations of a jury, rather than any other kind of group or organization, by virtue of the ways in which their members refer to and use materials and statements or voice arguments with regard to evidence given in court, etc.

In a similar way, Garfinkel (2002) refers to the concept of reflexivity when discussing the relationship between action and context.

Actions continuously generate the context within which they are produced and that shapes them. *Context* does not describe a clearly delineated environment where action occurs, rather context itself is *reflexively* constituted by virtue of the relationships between actions and the way in which participants specify aspects of identity, time, and space. Heritage (1984: 242) famously talks about actions as being at the same time "context-shaped" and "context-renewing," a statement that has been very influential in conversation analysis in particular.

A brief example might help clarify the relationship between action and context. Conventionally, a distinction is drawn between *instructions* and *instructed action*, whereby the former are seen as defining the production of the latter; actors are seen as following instructions, for example, to drill a hole in a wall. Through his tutorial exercises Garfinkel (2002: 197–217) demonstrated that instruction and instructed action are not independent from each other, but interdependent. Instructions never completely describe how an action, such as the drilling of a hole in a wall, is accomplished. They are necessarily incomplete and determined only in and through the practical accomplishment of instructed actions. When, in the process of the accomplishment of the instructed action, the 'intended' result is achieved, the actions implied in the instruction are specified; i.e., the actions implied in the instruction to drill the hole in a wall only emerge when the person actually does the drilling of the hole. In other words, the drilling of the hole constitutes the instruction; thus instruction and instructed action are in a reflexive relationship (Garfinkel 2002: 203–204).

## Unique Adequacy

When discussing Garfinkel's PhD dissertation, I suggested that his discussion of the difference between Parsons and Schutz, or the *theory of correspondence* and the *theory of congruency*, respectively, prefigured his later development of a *sociological attitude*, as he called it in his manuscript from 1948 (2006), which would allow him to overcome the Schutzian distinction of the actors' and the scientists' first and second order observations. The innovation of the ethnomethodological attitude lies in the postulate of *unique adequacy*, which demands the researchers to fully embed themselves into the social activities and acquire the competence and skills of the participants in order to be able to understand and pursue the activities just like the participants themselves. The principle of unique adequacy is based on the assumption that ethnomethodologists can make sense of others' activities only when they become *members*, i.e., participants, in the situation and experience it with their own bodies, just like those who usually work in and experience the situation. Ethnomethodologists are not concerned with explaining the organization of the situation by referring to sociological concepts and theories. Instead the motivation behind ethnomethodological research is to *adequately* describe how any competent participant (or member, in Garfinkel's terms) orients to the situation. It is worthwhile pointing out that when Garfinkel talked about *adequacy* in this context, he did not refer to the notion of "taking the role of the other" (Mead 1934), one of the key concepts in symbolic interactionism. In fact, even in his 1948 manuscript he had written that "the concept of 'seeing things from the actor's point of view,' even where the rules of procedure provide for sympathetic introspection, does not mean that the observer is 'taking the role of the other'" (Garfinkel 2006: 176). By 1948, he was already strongly critical of the interactionists' argument that adequacy could be achieved by virtue of imagining the other's attitude and orientation. Instead, at this time, Garfinkel suggested an alignment with Schutz's position, which implied a suspension of "the possibility of a community between the actor and the observer" (Garfinkel 1952: 112), because they approach situations with different attitudes, i.e., the natural attitude and the scientific attitude. Later, the postulate of unique adequacy would embody the fundamental shift in his concept of sociology, when he argued for a blending of the actor's and the observer's attitudes.

Ethnomethodology now differentiates between two kinds of unique adequacy that have emerged over the course of its history. The weak version of unique adequacy requires the researcher to develop an everyday and "vulgar" competence of the analyzed phenomenon:

Unique adequacy is identical with the requirement that for the analyst to recognize, or identify, or follow the development of, or describe phenomena of order in local production of coherent detail
the analyst must be *vulgarly* competent in the local production and
reflexively natural accountability of the phenomenon of order he [or
she] is 'studying' (Garfinkel and Wieder 1992: 182).

Thereby, Garfinkel and Wieder describe *vulgar competence* as the
knowledge that participants bring to bear in order to be able to continue to take part in the situation and to be seen as competent. The
researcher can acquire such competence, for example, by virtue of participant observation.

The strong version of unique adequacy particularly refers to the
way in which the analysis is presented. The methods of accounting for
and describing the organization the researcher uses to understand and
make sense of the participants' action are directly derived from the examined action. The ethnomethodologist focuses her/his analysis and
description on the methods that the participants deploy to pursue their
activities. This strong version of unique adequacy can be found in studies by ethnomethodologists who became jazz pianists (David Sudnow);
lawyers (Stacy Burns); and mathematicians (Eric Livingston), among
others. By acquiring the practical skills and competencies of professionals, ethnomethodologists conduct the activities of jazz pianists,
lawyers, and mathematicians themselves, rather than generate social
scientific descriptions of the same.

Unique adequacy clearly distinguishes the ethnomethodological
from the conventional sociological perspective. The differences between the two kinds of unique adequacy relate to the degree to which
the ethnomethodologist acquires the participants' competencies in the
respective field of studies and what kind of account and description
s/he produces based on her/his research. In this sense, the ethnomethodological principle of unique adequacy can be seen as a version of
the *emic* perspective that characterizes Goffman's studies (Rooke and
Kagioglou 2007); from this perspective, social order is made sense of

from the perspective of someone embedded in the organization and not from the *etic* perspective of a social scientist. The differentiation between weak and strong unique adequacy, however, also demonstrates that the principle is layered and that different studies require a different kind of unique adequacy.

## Endogenous Populations

As we have learned from examining Garfinkel's perspective on identity and groups, he did not consider the presence of particular people or persons constitutive for the existence of populations, rather he described them as *phenomena of order* that are made observable and intelligible through social action. He thereby referred, for example, to populations of waiting queues and traffic jams. He also used the term *phenomena of order* to describe the organization of some of the activities performed as part of his tutorial exercises, such as rhythmic clapping (Garfinkel 2002). In their analyses, Garfinkel and the ethnomethodologists are concerned with these populations and the actions that produce them in such ways that a particular social form becomes observable. In a well-known introduction to ethnomethodology, Eric Livingston (1987) used a crowd of people crossing a street as an example to explain different perspectives for examining the phenomenon. When observed from a bird's-eye perspective, the people created a triangular formation to avoid the traffic. However, the observer could move to a different perspective, from where s/he could focus on particular parts of the crowd and analyze particular local patterns that may interpret the organizational principles underlying people's crossing of the street. A third perspective would involve the ethnomethodologist becoming a member of the crowd and understanding the practices involved in crossing the street from within the crowd. This would allow her/him to experience, first-hand, the reflexive relationships between the participant's actions and those of other people in the crowd.

The shift of perspective from the bird's-eye to a perspective that provides the researcher access to the details of the practical organization allows the ethnomethodologist to examine *in situ* the organizational principles of the phenomenon. The analysis of autochthonous or endogenous populations demonstrates that they are independent from the presence of particular people and their social-demographic characteristics, and that they are, instead, constituted in and through the organization of members' practical action.

## Perspicuous Settings

When explaining why he had selected particular organizations, institutions and settings for his studies, Garfinkel (2002) referred to *perspicuous settings*. Perspicuous settings are domains where phenomena can be particularly clearly observed. In his definition of perspicuous settings, Garfinkel turned to "Sacks' gloss." In one of his studies, Sacks encountered the distinction between objects that can be possessed and therefore are *possessable*, and objects that already belong to somebody and therefore are *possessitives*. Sacks was then interested in how members in the everyday dealt with this distinction and, on reflection, mentioned to Garfinkel that the best way forward to find out was to find an organization whose task and function it was to determine the distinction between possessables and possessitives. He found such an organization in the Los Angeles Police Department, whose police officers regularly came across cars parked on the street with an unclear status; did somebody park the car there or had the car been left behind by car thieves? Ever since, "Sacks' Gloss" has been drawn on by ethnomethodologists as a method to look for settings that are particularly well suited to pursue a research question. Hence, when ethnomethodologists are interested in exploring particular practices, they look for a setting where these practices occur on a regular basis because they are key to the organization's work. Indeed, Garfinkel sometimes said he would read occupational handbooks to learn about the work activities particular occupations are concerned with in their daily work.

A concept related to Garfinkel and Wieder's (1992) discussion of perspicuous setting is Michael Lynch's (1993) discussion of *epistopics*.

In his seminal book *Scientific Practice and Ordinary Action* he explains that vernacular descriptions such as observation, discovery, explanation, or representation obscure that they are ordinary and mundane activities. Eric Laurier describes this in the following way:

> Ethnomethodology seeks a return to them as ordinary practices (e.g., birdwatchers observing eagles, neurologists redoing an experiment, economists measuring hospital efficiency, landscape gardeners imagining a new shrubbery, and explaining why one was so upset at work today) and in doing so remove the metaphysical aura of these grand topics (Laurier 2009: 632).

## Ethnomethodological Indifference

While ethnomethodological research may be interested in particular practices and seeks perspicuous settings when these practices can be found, it does not begin with theoretical concerns that are drawn from the existing social scientific corpus. It is also not concerned with the attitude and orientation of members with regard to a practical problem they have to deal with. In fact, ethnomethodologists are *indifferent* to these sociological interests, as well as to members' orientations (Garfinkel and Sacks 1970). Instead, their interest lies with understanding the phenomenon of order they observe in social situations. Thus, ethnomethodologists find out how participants in a particular situation systematically and "methodically" accomplish their actions pragmatically, through an action-by-action analysis of what an adequate next action is in a specific moment. Lynch (1993) referred to Garfinkel's (1967c) study of the co-workers coding information in a clinic. In his analysis Garfinkel was concerned with how the co-workers pursued this everyday activity and how they were treating information they were unable to attribute to particular codes. He argued that in such cases, the person who coded the information relied on "ad-hoc practices," such as the previously mentioned "et cetera" clause, to accomplish their work. This way of coding information sharply contradicted the methodology underlying conventional sociology, which needed to avoid ambiguities to make sure their findings were objective and generalizable.

Garfinkel's arguments and the principle of ethnomethodological indifference have implications for his understanding of the *methods* that ethnomethodologists deploy in their studies. In response to their critical view of traditional sociology, Garfinkel and other ethnomethodologists were often asked what they would consider to be *evidence* and how they would make decisions about the inclusion and exclusion of data as evidence in their studies (Garfinkel in Hill and Crittenden 1968). Rather than engaging in a discussion about validity and reliability, they argued for a different way to conduct social scientific research (Garfinkel and Sacks 1970). They proposed to define methods not in the way in which natural scientists would define it, i.e., as a standardized and objectively assessable process that guarantees the production of generalizable findings. Instead, ethnomethodologists argued in favor of analyzing the methods that participants themselves deploy in particular, concrete situations. Thereby, they suggested that close observations of the accomplishment of these methods would allow them to gain an understanding of how a particular action is produced in a certain way at a certain moment.

## Lebenswelt Pair

The notion of Lebenswelt Pair features quite prominently in Livingston's (1987) studies of mathematical proofs. His ethnomethodological analyses draw on Garfinkel and Sacks' (1970) distinction of practical action and formulation, such as instructed action and instruction, playing chess and the strategy of playing chess, or examining a patient and the patient's clinical record. With regards to Livingston's studies, the mathematical proof is made up of the formulation of the proof, i.e., the proof-account, and the lived-work of proving. The two parts of the pair are inextricably linked with each other. "The pairing—as one integral object, not as two distinct 'parts' circumstantially joined—is the 'proof' in and as the details of its own accomplishments" (Livingston 1987: 112).

Garfinkel discusses the concept of Lebenswelt Pair in his *Ethnomethodological Program* (2002) and then again a bit later in two journal articles (Garfinkel 2007b; Garfinkel and Liberman 2007). In these publications, he uses Lebenswelt Pair to explain ethnomethodology's concern with practices and processes, while at the same time showing how these practices are related to formulations and accounts. As an example of such a Lebenswelt Pair, he referred to the distinction of "measure" and the process of "measuring." He argued that while sociology was often looking for differences between measures, such as differences between social classes, it ignored the practices that needed to be accomplished to arrive at those measures, i.e., the practices of measuring including the gathering of data, the deployment of statistical tools and technologies, etc. To give another example, grades in schools are used by sociologists as indicators of pupils' achievements. Grades are compared and investigations are conducted to identify reasons underlying variations between pupils' performance, for example, by generating correlations with pupils' socio-demographic and economic background, their gender, etc. In Garfinkel's view, the focus on measures rather than on the practices of measuring meant that sociology lost what is at the core of the enterprise, i.e., the organization of practice through which a "social fact," such as grades in school, is assessed.

Garfinkel argued for a shift in focus from measures that transform qualities, such as achievements in school, into quantitative indicators, to the practices of measuring. There are different ways in which sociologists can study this process of *commensuration*, i.e., the transforming of qualities into quantities (cf. Stevens and Espeland 2005). For example, an ethnographer can observe and make fieldnotes on this process. Thereby, s/he creates a set of documents, i.e., ethnographic fieldnotes, collections of sketches and photographs, etc. that exist alongside the certificates that show pupils' achievement in school as "grades." Both documents, the ethnographer's description and the certificates, are in an asymmetric relationship to each other because the ethnographic account of the process allows the researcher, to some extent, to reconstruct and understand the way in which the achievement was measured. Yet, when starting with the certificates that mark pupils' achievement in school, it is impossible to understand the process of grading that is described in the ethnographic fieldnotes. In other words, social scientists who base their analyses on reports, transcripts or other kinds of codes that are supposed to stand for members' practices reduce the concrete situation to such an extent that they create a gap in the literature, rather than filling one; they utterly ignore the "missing what" (Lynch 1993)[5], i.e., the practical knowledge and competences that participants deploy in situations.[6]

Another well-known example of a Lebenswelt Pair that Garfinkel (2002) and his students elaborated on was the relationship between instructions and instructed actions. Instructions like those that come with flat-pack furniture are unavoidably incomplete, because they describe the various phases or stages in the assembly of a piece of furniture, but fail to describe the detailed practices involved in the assembly process. These detailed practices are the 'instructed' actions that draw on the instructions as resources, but whichfor the completion of the task of assembling the furniture require a filling in of 'blanks'—those practices that need to be undertaken but are not covered by the instructions. In the process of their accomplishment these practices constitute the drawings and sketches that have come with the furniture as "instructions," and in turn through the process of assembling the furniture with the help of the "instructions" the practices become intelligible as "instructed actions." This example reveals how ethnomethodologists deal with the asymmetric relationship of the elements that make up a Lebenswelt Pair. Instead of analyzing the instructions, ethnomethodological studies shift the focus to the practical accomplishment and achievement of instructions. Their analyses in various technology-rich environments have made important contributions to the technical sciences, such as Computer Supported Cooperative Work (CSCW) or Human Computer Interaction (HCI).

As Garfinkel continued to explicate the ethnomethodological program and thereby further develop the ethnomethodological perspective, he gradually distanced himself from early ethnomethodology which was more clearly influenced by Schutz's phenomenology. The tutorial exercises that were key to Garfinkel's doctoral research in the 1950s aimed to make the taken-for-granted knowledge as the basis for the social order of situations, observable and experience-able. In the course of the development of the ethnomethodological program, Garfinkel (1996, 2002) became increasingly interested in investigating the experience of endogenous and autochthonous organization of social situations. The shift in Garfinkel's more recent studies to the embodied practices through which order is produced and experienced marks a distancing from, or at least a new way of interpreting, i.e., a "misreading," of Schutz's phenomenology.

Lynch (1993: 133–141) talked about the early ethnomethodology that was built on Schutz's conceptions of *worlds* and *cognitive style* as proto-ethnomethodology. This proto-ethnomethodology "did not emphasize the concrete embodiment of local action" (Lynch 1993: 137), and was therefore sometimes seen in relationship to concurrent developments in the cognitive sciences. In particular, discussions of the breaching experiments seemed to suggest that Garfinkel had an interest in actors' cognitive orientation and adherence to tacit rules or norms in situations. However, this interpretation of Garfinkel's demonstrations and early studies overlooked, as Lynch (1993: 141) observed, that Garfinkel "demonstrates how these ["background expectancies," "common understandings"] are intertwined with 'scenic' features of commonplace settings rather than founded in a normative or cognitive space" (Lynch 1993: 141, Fn 58). This interest in embodied practices and its situatedness in material and visual locales is of particular significance for the development of what have become known as *ethnomethodological studies of work*.

## Ethnomethods and Social Theory

By developing the ethnomethodological program, Garfinkel (1996; 2002) accomplished two important tasks: first, he gave those interested in ethnomethodological studies a theoretical and analytic framework that allowed them to conduct research aimed at revealing *ethnometh-*

*ods*, i.e., actions that observably-and-reportably exhibit order; second, he demonstrated the important contribution that ethnomethodology has made to social theory (cf. Helm 1989).

With regards to ethnomethodology's contribution to sociology, its respecification of reflexivity as a fundamental characteristic of action is worthwhile highlighting here once more. Through his studies Garfinkel demonstrated that sociologists' research interests lay in phenomena that are constituted through the reflexivity of interaction between the people under scrutiny. In contrast to the natural sciences, sociologists ascribe meaning to phenomena that is inseparable from the meaning that the participants under study ascribe to them (cf. Wilson and Zimmerman 1979). By understanding reflexivity in this way, sociology not only differentiates itself from the natural sciences, but also from behaviorism, which that attempts to describe the organization of human action as independent from the ways in which participants themselves orient to it.

Reflexivity is the basis for ethnomethodology's explication of the methods through which participants themselves accomplish the phenomenon of order. For ethnomethodologists, "[T]o imagine an unreflexive action would be like imagining a sound without amplitude" (Lynch 2000a: 45). This is true for actions in the everyday world as well as for sociological descriptions (Macbeth 2001).

Garfinkel argued that there is order in the production of each and every action, and this order does not require the deployment of a formal-analytic framework. Participants continuously analyze a situation and produce action in alignment with the emerging organization. The prime example that ethnomethodologists and conversation analysts refer to is the organization of talk, i.e., the "turn-taking machine" that participants deploy in conversation (Sacks, Schegloff, and Jefferson 1974). For example, the *adjacency pair*, made up of question and answer, reflexively emerges from the way in which the second utterance, the answer constitutes the first action as a question and thus becomes an answer to that question. Moreover, the second action, the answer, not only treats the first action intelligibly as a question, but also provides the framework for a subsequent utterance, for example, another question or an expression of gratitude, "thank you" (cf. Heritage 1984).

Participants are able to organize conversations or interviews in this way, not because a sociologist has provided them with a formal-analytic framework, but because they analyze each other's actions moment-by-moment and orient to them by producing appropriate next actions. Participants in conversation are themselves conversation analysts who examine each turn of talk and attend to it with an appropriate next turn. Or, in other words, the order of the situation does not rely on a sociological theory, rather participants themselves momentarily accomplish its orderliness (Helm 1989; Wilson and Zimmerman 1979). Ethnomethodological research and maybe, up to now, in a more influential way conversation analysis, has investigated this accomplishment of orderliness. Heritage (1984: 254–260) called the structure underlying this accomplishment of orderliness the "architecture of intersubjectivity." He, as well as the now enormous body of conversation analytic research, unpacks the building blocks of inter-subjectivity by investigating how participants themselves, moment-by-moment, orient to and align with an ongoing course of action (Heritage 2009). Thus, those pursuing Garfinkel's program of research to understand how participants bring about intersubjectivity in situations make fundamental contributions to social theory by respecifying the question of social order. They explore different ways of "theorizing" (Blum 1974), and their analyses focus on the ways in which participants deploy theories of action and meaning in concrete, rather than abstract, situations (cf. Heritage 1984, 2009, 2010).

Garfinkel's ethnomethodological program has had important implications for the way in which social theory is conceived and theorizing is done. Indeed, as Rawls (1989b: 4) observes, "an ethnomethodological perspective holds the potential to clarify some rather important issues in social theory." Formal-analytic sociologists are preoccupied with making historically comparable arguments. Their prime concern is with the comparability of sociological propositions over time and often, also, across cultures. Ethnomethodology's principal interest is in understanding the organization of concrete events. It considers the description of social phenomena as "reflexively related to the understanding and beliefs of the members of the group being studied" (Wilson and Zimmerman 1979: 64). Hence, such descriptions, including those produced by sociological theory, are "historically situated" (ibid.).

Wilson and Zimmerman (1979) explored the notion of historical situatedness of sociological theory by drawing on Weber's *ideal type of bureaucracy* as an example. Rather than trying to identify cases that have the same features as the ideal type of a bureaucracy, they suggested that the point of Weber's concept is to offer researchers a model with which they can compare their empirical data. They can examine how close to or distant from the ideal type their empirical data are. Thus, researchers who conduct their studies historically situate their findings about the features of a bureaucracy, rather than using the ideal type as a general concept that is removed from specific historical and cultural circumstances. This view of theory as being not "trans-historical" (Wilson and Zimmerman 1979: 63–67), but situated historically and culturally, is alien to formal-analytic sociology because it does not lead to propositions that can be added to a general, theoretical framework.

Instead, in ethnomethodological research, theory derives directly from concrete instances of social order and provides the basis for further research as well as, on occasions, allowing for the generation of testable hypotheses (Wilson and Zimmerman 1979: 72). The basic assumption is that ethnomethods, such as the turn-taking system in conversation, organize action and that this organization is independent of historical and cultural influences. Ethnomethodologists reveal this organization of interaction and are not interested in examining the content of talk. They study "the mechanisms by which members of society construct and sustain those meaningful accounts out of which sociological phenomena are constituted, rather than sociological phenomena themselves" (Wilson and Zimmerman 1979: 75). Ethnomethodology, however, does not want to be an alternative sociology, yet it recognizes that the accounts of order it produces, are, themselves, reflexively embedded within the context in which they are produced. Whether or not this means that ethnomethodological concepts also are historically situated and not invariant, remains to be seen.

# Chapter 7

# Ethnomethodological Studies of Work

Garfinkel developed his interest in the organization of work before he published his edited collection *Ethnomethodological Studies of Work* (Garfinkel 1986). In fact, already in the 1950s and 1960s, Garfinkel had analyzed work practice and the practical reasoning of actors who used their knowledge of an organization to come to decisions about their actions, in his studies of jurors in their deliberations (Garfinkel 1967f) and of personnel in clinics (Garfinkel 1967h).

Before Garfinkel gathered data for these studies, he completed and submitted his doctoral research and worked on a research project at Princeton. The project was administered by Wilbert Moore,[1] whom Garfinkel knew from a project he had been involved with a decade earlier. After he had submitted his MA thesis, Garfinkel had joined a research project Moore was conducting in Bastrop, Texas, which was concerned with social change in the town engendered by a temporary military industry. Garfinkel presumed that Moore would possibly be disappointed that he had conducted field-studies rather than using institutional measures, as suggested by the project leader. Yet, he was sure that such detailed observations of the social activities in Bastrop were more insightful than quantitative measures. Despite the apparent differences in their approaches to this study, Garfinkel seemed to have left a good impression on Moore, who hired him to work on a prestigious Organizational Behavior Project funded by the Ford Foundation. His contribution to the project involved the organization of colloquia and conferences, as well as the writing of research grant applications and the supervision of students in seminars at the University of Princeton (Rawls 2008b).

Garfinkel's work at Princeton coincided with the beginning of the computerization of work processes and the deployment of computer

*Harold Garfinkel: The Creation and Development of Ethnomethodology* by Dirk vom Lehn. 119–132. © 2013 UVK Verlagsgesellschaft mbH; additional material for English edition © 2014 Left Coast Press, Inc. All rights reserved.

systems in organizations. Universities and other kinds of organizations had purchased large computer systems and were establishing computing centers that social scientists and others could use to analyze surveys and databases. From the 1970s onwards, social scientists considered the informatization of organization as the beginning of a new era and a transformation of society that, more recently, has been described as the "information society," "post-capitalist society," or "post-industrial society" (Bell 1973; Toffler 1981). At the same time, new theories of information and communication were being developed in mathematics and other disciplines, such as models of the transmission and exchange of information (Shannon and Weaver 1949), that later influenced the development of theories of human communication (Bateson and Ruesch 1951). In sociology, these developments became apparent when quantitative research methods gained in importance because computer systems could now analyze the huge amounts of data created by surveys of large populations. The procedures and methods underlying this emerging body of studies were based on the categorization and coding of actions, people, and events, as well as on theories of representation, arguing that meaning is lodged in symbols and words.

Garfinkel recognized that the formalizing of information proposed by mathematicians and theories of information was inadequate to analyze and understand human communication because the formalization abstracted from the indexicality of language in use. When he began to work on the Organizational Behavior Project, Garfinkel had not yet formally developed the concepts of *indexicality* and *reflexivity*. However, he had already noticed the shortcomings of the theorizing about social action in *Seeing Sociologically* (Garfinkel 2006 [1948]). He picked up this topic again in manuscripts that he wrote while working at Princeton, one of which has recently been published as "Memo #3" in the book *Toward a Sociological Theory of Information* (2008 [1952]). In this book, Garfinkel developed a position that continued his line of thought on communication and interaction that could already be found in *Seeing Sociologically* (2006 [1948]). He now also pursued the question as to how it was possible that, despite the indexicality of information, actors align their perspectives and interact with each other unproblematically (Garfinkel 2008 [1952]).

As demonstrated in previous chapters, traditional sociologists considered indexicality as problematic and deployed theoretical models and systems of categories to deal with it. They presumed that information was objectively represented through symbols. However, already in the 1940s Garfinkel was convinced that meaning was not lodged in symbols such as written or spoken words, but that it was constituted in social processes and interaction produced in concrete situations (Rawls 2008b; Thielmann 2012). Actors experience the world they inhabit as coherent because they produce objects in interaction with others. This coherence of the experience of the world and of the ways in which objects are made sense of in interaction with others is the basis for the constitution of social order.

Although in the 1940s and 1950s Garfinkel had been concerned with the interactional constitution of objects and the social production of meaning, he only became interested in the significance of the fine details of action and their organization much later in his career, when he cooperated with Harvey Sacks on the analysis of recorded talk and conversation (Thielmann 2012). In his introduction to *Ethnomethodological Studies of Work* Garfinkel (1986: vi) wrote that in light of his examination of audio-recordings of conversation, Sacks was sure "that the local production of social order existed as an orderliness of conversational practices." By virtue of the concerted analysis of audio-recordings such as those collected at the Los Angeles Suicide Prevention Center, Garfinkel and Sacks became increasingly aware of the importance of the fine detailed organization of social interaction. In their further development of ethnomethodology and conversation analysis, Garfinkel and Sacks, as well as their students, focused on the detailed organization of action and interaction in work settings.

When Garfinkel turned his interest to the organization of work, a large corpus of research on the sociology of work already existed. Since the 1950s, the Chicago School of Sociology, Symbolic Interactionism (Blumer 1954, 1969), and, in particular, Everett Hughes (Heath 1984;

Hughes 1951, 1984) had developed a program of ethnographic research on the organization of work and occupations. For example, in *Boys in White*, Howard Becker and colleagues (1961) published an ethnography of student culture in a medical school, and Becker (1951) had also undertaken studies of the jazz music scene that revealed how people displayed their membership in the jazz scene. This study also analyzed the attitudes of members of the jazz scene and the role conflicts they encountered as fathers and professionals due to their participation in the scene. In Garfinkel's view these analyses did not go far enough, because they failed to study the phenomenon of "making jazz," i.e., the practices through which people play jazz music and thus generated what was at the heart of the jazz scene. He argued that Becker and colleagues provided interesting observations in the life-world of jazz musicians, but that fairly little was learned about the practices through which people became jazz musicians and members of the jazz scene.

By focusing on the practice of making jazz music instead, ethnomethodology is able to analyze phenomena of social order in jazz music making that otherwise remain hidden behind sociological concepts. Such studies of the practice of jazz piano playing were conducted by David Sudnow, an ethnomethodologist with a PhD from Berkeley. Before he undertook his research on the organization of piano playing, he had become well known for his studies of hospital work and the ways in which dying patients were treated by members of staff. By examining how staff oriented to patients, Sudnow found that, "a patient is treated essentially as a corpse, though perhaps still 'clinically' and 'biologically' alive" (Sudnow 1967: 74). In cases where this happened, i.e., where personnel were treating a patient as dead, biologically death became more likely. Sudnow followed this with studies on piano playing (Sudnow 1979) and video gaming (Sudnow 2000). His research on piano playing was concerned with the practical production of action, i.e., the hitting of a key on a piano, and the importance of the temporal organization underlying each action. It uncovered the practices and observable-and-reportable competences actors undertake which result in music. While in traditional sociology of music the practical making of music escapes the sociologist, in ethnomethodological studies, the music playing is put at the heart of the research. Thus, ethnomethodologists can show how musicians practically make music and are often able to play together, even when they have only just met.

By focusing on the practices through which particular kinds of social order are produced in work places, Garfinkel and his students began to elaborate on the details of practical work. Some of this research has been published in Garfinkel's *Ethnomethodological Studies of Work* (1986) whereby the contributions to this book take a very wide view of "work"; the book includes studies of martial arts, the transcribing of lectures, alchemy and other activities, as well as Garfinkel and Sacks' well known programmatic paper "On formal structures of practical action" (cf. 1970).

Some of Garfinkel's students have gone on to make important contributions to the emergence of new sociological areas of research. One of his best-known students is Michael Lynch, who is today Professor of Science and Technology Studies at Cornell University. As Garfinkel's doctoral student, Lynch developed an interest in the social studies of science; his PhD dissertation was later published as *Art and Artefact in Laboratory Science: A Study of Shop Work and Shop Talk in a Laboratory* (Lynch 1985). Together with Garfinkel, he published two very influential articles that examined the organization of the *shop work* of natural scientists in research laboratories, as well as the importance of *shop talk*, i.e., the naturally occurring conversations of scientists while they conducted their studies.

In their research, Garfinkel, Lynch and Livingston (1981) subjected written documents, field observation and audio-recordings of shop talk in research laboratories to detailed analysis, in order to understand the organization of the practice of doing science. This organization became observable in the actions of the participants in the research laboratories. Astronomers, for example, *intertwined*[2] action with technologies to objects such as a pulsating star called "pulsar." Garfinkel, Lynch, and Livingston's analyses demonstrated that pulsars and other scientific objects are not natural or physical phenomena that exist independently from social action, but that the social organization of action in laboratories is critical for the coming into existence of such objects.

Together with his colleagues Lynch and Livingston, Garfinkel (1983) explored the processes through which such scientific activities were accomplished. They showed that for the practical purposes of these activities, scientists conducted mundane practices that are incompletely and insufficiently captured by idioms like "scientific methods." Ethnomethodological analyses are basic research, or in Lynch and colleagues' terminology (1983), the *foundational inquiries* that help to analyze the locally observable-and-reportable sequences of action in ordinary, discipline-specific work. Thereby, they proposed that practical actions are specific to particular disciplines and suggested that such actions are designed to make visible the temporary production of the contents that make up those disciplines (ibid.).

Ethnomethodological analyses of shop talk and work in laboratories has revealed that scientists rely on ordinary, mundane competences and practices to pursue their work. These everyday competences and practices also allow scientists to revisit their work and materials, and thereupon revise the arguments that they originally used to explain their findings, if they encounter problems or even failures in their actions.

When looking at scientific articles in journals or at scientific textbooks, we find descriptions of the processes of science work. These formalized instructions and reports of scientific methods and observed events fundamentally differ from the concrete work of scientists in actual laboratories. These differences have been brought to the fore by a doctoral student of Mike Lynch, Dusan Bjelic (1996, 2003), who conducted a study of Galileo's famous pendulum experiments using Galileo's original descriptions of them. When Galileo conducted his experiments in 1602, he produced detailed documents in which he delineated the process through which he came to his findings about the period of the pendulum. With his experiments he aimed to show that the period for which a pendulum swings is independent from the width of the swing.

In his study, Bjelic used Galileo's detailed documentation of the research process, methods and the ways in which he used instruments and technologies, as instructions to conduct the very same experiment as the famous seventeenth century scientist. Bjelic's interest in this study, however, was not to prove or disprove the existence of a "natural law," but to experience the practical action that was required to conduct the experiments. In the process, he noticed problems that were not reported in Galileo's documents. By deploying methods and accounts for these observations, such as "ad hoc" and "in vivo" explanations and practical solutions that Bjelic had to produce in the process of the experiments, he was able to restore the order and organization of the experiment.

Garfinkel (2002) discussed similar experiments in chapter nine of *Ethnomethodology's Program* where he developed the distinction between *classic accountability* and *natural accountability*. *Classic accountability* referred to the possibility that scientists can produce *post-hoc* explanations of their actions and procedures that deviate from textbook instructions. Such explanations are produced after the experiments have been conducted and can be found in reports and textbooks that describe the experiments; *natural accountability* involves explanations that scientists produce in the process of doing the experiments, to explain problems and deviations from procedure and, thus, find practical solutions in situ. These natural accounts of procedures and problems are similar to those explanations that people ordinarily produce in the everyday to continue ongoing sequences of action, even when problems arise.

Ethnomethodological studies of science have made important contributions to our understanding of the relationship between knowledge about scientific procedure as communicated in textbooks, and the practical knowledge that is required to conduct scientific work. For example, while textbooks describe clearly defined, linear processes of scientific procedure and thereby differentiate distinct phases or stages in the scientific process, ethnomethodological analyses show that science work is subject to contingencies of the situations in which it is conducted. In this sense, textbooks and chapters describing scientific methods and procedures are ideals that cannot be found in the reality of scientific practice.

Ethnomethodological analyses explore the relationships between the ideals of scientific practice and the actual, situated and embodied practices of scientific practice. For example, ethnomethodological research has investigated how instructions are transformed in their deployment by participants and become intelligible as instructed action; it has also explored how the transformation of instructions to instructed action is subject to unanticipated events that the participants address *in situ* by virtue of practical action that is not covered by instruction manuals and textbooks of practice (cf. Garfinkel 2002). Lynch and colleagues (1983) argued, for example, that scientists become "local historians" when they notice a mistake or error in the process of their experiments, to understand what went wrong and to restore the order of the experiment. While theories of scientific practice assume that processes move forward gradually, ethnomethodological research has demonstrated that in their practice, scientists also look back at past events and actions to understand and correct them in order to allow for an experiment to continue. Furthermore, their detailed analyses of scientific practice has revealed the organization of the noticing of and response to scientific discoveries (Sormani 2011).

Bjelic (1996: 410) denoted the distinction between theory and practice as a *Lebenswelt Pair*: "The first part of the Lebenswelt Pair is the formal structure of science as an accomplished object as presented in textbooks and journals in the form of theorems, hypotheses, logic of inquiry, experimental descriptions, data, etc. The second part of the Lebenswelt Pair is the actual and unexplained production of tacit discovering structures." While there are multiple descriptions of the first part of the Lebenswelt Pair, the second part of the Lebenswelt Pair of science is often ignored. Hence, scientists assume that scientific objects such as pulsars exist independently from scientific procedures. This assumption is based on scientific reports that abstract from the ordinary work involved in the discovery of the object as well as the shop talk and the action that the participants produce in the laboratories. It requires scientists to ignore the activities and events in the laboratory and see the object as part of nature. Garfinkel's ethnomethodology, therefore, remained agnostic or "indifferent" to the concept of 'natural objects' (consistent with the idea of *ethnomethodological indifference* discussed in the chapter What is Ethnomethodology?), as these are criteria that the sociologist is not necessarily equipped to adjudicate. Instead, Garfinkel treated scientific discoveries as *cultural objects*, paying no heed to the concept of *truthfulness* in science. In a certain sense, this is a combination of Karl Popper's (2002 [1934]) *Logic of Scientific Inquiry*, which states that all scientific discovery is constantly subject to reinterpretation and revision, and W. I. Thomas' (1967 [1928]) theorem, whereby if humans treat things as real, they are real in their consequences. Garfinkel noted that scientists can reconstruct by examining documents, reports and memories of the scientific process (Garfinkel et al. 1981), and as such, the idea of 'truth' or 'scientific knowledge' is pinned to the mutual, social accomplishment of 'scientific facts' by those socially sanctioned to discuss science, i.e., scientists, and what they come to agree upon when examining and/or re-examining their findings and data. We might note that this theme is quite heavily explored in the work of Bruno Latour, who does not identify himself as an ethnomethodologist, although he does credit Garfinkel as being one of the most significant sociological thinkers of his time (Latour 1987, 2005).

Ethnomethodologists are not concerned with the ontology of natural scientists, but instead they analyze the ways in which knowledge is generated through the intertwining of practical action with material, visual, and other resources. They focus on the methods that scientists actually deploy when they gather and examine data. They argue that *artifacts* become accountable objects by virtue of the use of these methods in concrete situations arising in laboratories. By reflecting on the activities conducted in the research process, Lynch and colleagues (Lynch 1985; Lynch, Garfinkel, and Livingstone 1983: 224; Lynch 1993) suggested that this *members' archaeology* allowed for the "discovering" of the object. Scientifically produced objects or artifacts can be traced back to actions and descriptions that scientists produce and that, therefore, can be investigated.

Social constructivists would argue that scientific findings are social constructions (Knorr-Cetina 1981; Knorr-Cetina and Mulkay 1983). However, there is an intrinsic metaphysical distinction in this line of reasoning that stipulates the world is in two parts: the world that is experienced and described or interpreted by science/scientists, and the world that 'really exists'. As with all things metaphysical, there is little chance of settling this debate, and ethnomethodologists are not particularly interested in abstract philosophy. Instead, ethnomethodological studies of science shift the focus to the practical action of scientists, through which they produce objects and theoretical constructs in concrete situations in laboratories. Thus, ethnomethodology avoids philosophical debates and, instead, is able to study the arguments and practices that make mundane actions intelligible as scientific practice (Lynch et al. 1983).

Garfinkel and his students and colleagues were aware of the significance of their arguments for philosophical discussions about the reality of scientific objects. They published their article describing the natural sciences under the title "Discovering sciences" in the journal *Philosophy of the Social Sciences* (Garfinkel, Lynch, and Livingston 1981). The article encouraged the professor of physics and historian of science Gerald Holton (1981) to publish a comment to the article describing Garfinkel as a "dangerous" man, by alluding to the fact that ethnomethodological research questions and challenges the objectivity of scientific knowledge that has been produced by scientific methods and procedures. Rather than seeing themselves as challenging scientific knowledge, ethnomethodologists are indifferent to the quality of scientific knowledge and, instead, consider scientific discoveries as cultural objects that are produced through mundane practices and methods and in reference to instructions provided by philosophers of science (Sormani, Philippe, González-Martínez, and Bovet 2011).

Garfinkel and Lynch's ethnomethodological analysis of the work conducted in the laboratories of astronomers made important and influential contributions to the development of *laboratory studies* in the 1980s, and the recent emergence of the sociology of science and technology (Hacket et al. 2008). Most recently, analysis of work in stock exchanges and financial markets has drawn on such ethnomethodological studies of work and has begun to invigorate research on the work practices in financial markets and in dealing rooms (Knorr-Cetina and Preda 2006; Knorr-Cetina and Bruegger 2002; MacKenzie 2005).

Today, the development of the sociology of science is often ascribed to *Actor–Network Theory* (ANT) and the influential studies by Latour, Law, Woolgar, and others (Latour 1987; Law 1991; Woolgar and Lynch 1990). Yet ethnomethodological studies offer a very different perspective on scientific work by examining the concrete work practices of scientists in their laboratories that produce scientific knowledge. Furthermore, these studies of science work provided the starting point for the more recent development of Garfinkel's (2002) *hybrid studies of work*, a program of research that would take a distinctive form as it became integrated with the pedagogies and practices of music, law, medicine, mathematics, and so on.

## Hybrid Studies of Work

When Garfinkel conceived of *ethnomethodological studies of work*, he defined "work" broadly, as shown by the content of his 1986 book of the same name, and radicalized the relationship between the practices of ethnomethodologists and the practices of those they observe and participate in. He later (2002) denoted the intertwining of research and practice as *hybrid* and described the studies of work and technology in action as *hybrid studies of work*. Nowadays such analyses are undertaken by researchers with a good understanding of the work practices in the setting under scrutiny. They focus on the practical problems that personnel deal with in their day-to-day work and explain the knowledge and competences that these personnel take for granted when they go about their business.

Considering the close link between research and practice suggested by Garfinkel's hybrid studies approach, it is not surprising that those concerned with the development and innovation of technologies and work practice have become interested in ethnomethodology. Since the 1980s, a considerable number of ethnomethodologists, therefore, not only hold faculty positions at universities in the USA, the UK, Japan, and elsewhere, but also industrial research laboratories such as those of Microsoft, Hewlett Packard, IBM, and PARC(Xerox) employ ethnomethodologists to support innovation and product development. As members of larger research teams, ethnomethodologists conduct detailed analyses of work practice to inform the development of new technologies. This close relationship between ethnomethodological research and technology development is grounded in Garfinkel's and other ethnomethodologists' interest in the details of work practices and their organization.

The interest of technology developers in ethnomethodology comes from the intertwining of research and practice, as well as from the novel forms of description that Garfinkel and other ethnomethodologists have developed. As discussed in previous chapters, Garfinkel demanded that analyses produce *uniquely adequate* descriptions, not to be generated to contribute to the sociological corpus of literature, but to be recognizable by practitioners. Garfinkel therefore argued for the merging of ethnomethodology and work practice by turning ethnomethodological descriptions of work into practical instructions for work. The possibility of such a close relationship between research and practice requires that ethnomethodologists acquire competencies and knowledge that come very close to the knowledge and competencies of the personnel whose practices are the subject of their studies.

Because, for the participants, the practices are observable and intelligible, ethnomethodologists can describe them in ways that are also adequate in the eyes of the participants themselves. These ethnomethodological descriptions, therefore, can also become relevant for the practitioners because they can use them to reflect on their work. Garfinkel described this relevance for practitioners as "topical relevance to the parties," an ethnomethodological principle that he explains with regard to the use of maps in way finding. In his view, maps are not suitable to understand the work involved in finding a way. "The traveler's work of consulting the map is an unavoidable detail in the lived, on-goingly, in-its-course, first time through, traveling body's way-finding journey that the map is consulted to get done" (Garfinkel 2002: 130). In other words, actions can be described in a way useful for practitioners only when the descriptions are done in ways that reflect the concrete circumstances and the practical reasoning with which the actions have been produced.

Hybrid studies of work have influenced the development of related programs of research such as ethnomethodological ethnographies of work and ethnomethodologically informed ethnographies (Harper 1997; Randall, Harper, and Rouncefield 2000); workplace studies (Engestrom and Middleton 1998; Heath and Luff 2000; Luff, Hindmarsh, and Heath 2000); and video-based studies of work and organization (Llewellyn and Hindmarsh 2010; Szymanski and Whalen 2011). These studies demonstrate how detailed analyses of activities conducted by specialists and experts with particular, workplace-specific knowledge and competencies can contribute to ongoing debates in the sociology of work and organizations, as well as to ethnomethodological studies interested in how objects, tools, and technologies are embedded within social action and interaction. Before I turn to the contributions and influences of ethnomethodology on wider sociological questions and discussions, in the following chapter I explore the relationship between ethnomethodology and sociology.

# Chapter 8

# Ethnomethodology and Sociology

At the beginning of this book I mentioned the sometimes difficult relationship between ethnomethodology and sociology. It was noted that well-known social scientists, such as Ernest Gellner and Lewis Coser, saw nothing of value in the ethnomethodological program. And, at times ethnomethodologists did not help their standing within sociology when they "formulated many of its [ethnomethodology's] own notions partly in polemical opposition to certain presuppositions of the main stream of conventional sociology" (Wilson and Zimmerman 1979: 53). Suggestions, however, that Garfinkel and ethnomethodology would have no interest in, and no contribution to make to, sociological debates and sociological theory are misguided. As I have demonstrated in reference to Garfinkel's analyses in the 1940s and 1950s, Garfinkel had an immense interest in sociological theory and in foundational sociological questions such as the question of social order. This early interest in sociological theory was reflected in Garfinkel's description of his excitement when opening his copy of Parsons' *The Social Structure of Action* (1937) in the late 1930s: "[H]e says that he can still remember sitting in the backyard fingering the book, smelling the newness of its pages" (Garfinkel in Rawls 2002: 13).

Despite his admiration for Parsons, Garfinkel's later studies were littered with discussions that strove to differentiate ethnomethodology from traditional sociology which, throughout the 1960s and 1970s, was dominated to a large extent by Parsonian and Neo-Parsonian approaches to theory and methods. Recently, Garfinkel clarified the sociological roots of his critique of traditional sociology, in other words, his reassessment of Durkheim's *social facts*. His efforts to clarify ethnomethodology's relationship to sociology were supported by Anne Rawls' intensive reevaluation of Durkheim and, in particular, his stud-

*Harold Garfinkel: The Creation and Development of Ethnomethodology* by Dirk vom Lehn. 133–146. © 2013 UVK Verlagsgesellschaft mbH; additional material for English edition © 2014 Left Coast Press, Inc. All rights reserved.

ies of *Elementary Forms of Religious Life* (Rawls 2009a). Rawls explains that Durkheim's book is not so much concerned with primitive belief-systems, but rather lays the foundation for a sociology focusing on social practice.

Rawls' reevaluation of Durkheim, coupled with Garfinkel's (2002) "working out" of Durkheim's *Aphorism*, provides us with a starting point to consider the relationship between ethnomethodology and sociology. This chapter briefly explores how ethnomethodology stands with regard to a few selected sociological approaches, principally interactionism; Goffman's sociology; conversation analysis; and phenomenological sociology.

## Ethnomethodology and Interactionism

Sociological textbooks often frame ethnomethodology and symbolic interactionism as if they were pursuing almost the same research agenda (Appelrouth and Edles 2008; Fulcher and Scott 2007; Giddens 2009). The implied identity of ethnomethodology and interactionism originates from a joint preference for the actor's perspective over the researcher's perspective, and from their joint interest in the process of interaction and communication. Intensive analyses and comparisons of both sociological perspectives, however, show that they are based on different orientations to the *interaction order* explored below.

While highlighting here the differences between ethnomethodology and interactionism, I do not intend to drive a wedge between these two distinct, but related, perspectives on studying social action. Indeed, despite some fundamental differences between ethnomethodology and interactionism, their studies have common concerns, such as their interest in *practice* as a phenomenon. This common concern with practice that is present in ethnomethodology and interactionism derives from their intellectual relationship with the philosophy of pragmatism, developed in Chicago from the late nineteenth century (Joas 1993; Simpson 2009). The emergence of interactionism from pragmatism is well documented. Relatively little is known, however, about ethnomethodology's relationship to pragmatist concepts and theories. Superficially seen, the theoretical and conceptual developments within pragmatism seem alien to the empirically oriented approach proposed by Garfinkel. Yet pragmatism and Garfinkel's ethnomethodology share a number of concerns: First, both investigate how actors experience and make sense of the world in and through their, *in situ* and *in vivo*, actions. Second, they both imply in their research that obstacles and resistance to action are important to the actor's experience of the world; and third, they assume that the meaning of language, action, and objects arises in, and through, social interaction.

When Garfinkel began his studies for a PhD at Harvard in the 1940s, he worked on a manuscript that now has been published as *Seeing Sociologically* (2006 [1948]). In this book, he positioned his sociological perspective with regards to contemporary sociology, including the interactionist sociology that emerged in light of the analyses by the Chicago philosophers and sociologists, such as William James, Charles Sanders Peirce, John Dewey, and George Herbert Mead. From the 1940s onward, the pragmatist school of thought, and, in sociology, symbolic interactionism, developed an alternative to the functionalist paradigm. The pragmatists strove to replace the distinction of external physical and internal cognitive reality that dominated the contemporary scientific discourse. Pragmatists argued that the assumption of an independent, physical "matter" and an individual "mind" as two distinct objects was wrong and proposed that they should be viewed as being connected through practical action.[1] They argued for a reflexive relationship between the existence of the world and the experience of the world; the world only exists when it is experienced and one can only have an experience if there is a world that can be experienced. Dewey and Bentley described this relationship as a transaction that demands, "[…] the seeing together, when research requires it, of what before had been seen in separations and held severally apart" (Dewey and Bentley 1976 in Emirbayer and Maynard 2011: 226).

Mead (1934: 129) illustrated the reflexive relationship between the world and experience by saying that grass only becomes seen as "edible" because there is an organism, e.g., a cow, that is able to digest it. In a similar way, pragmatists explained that objects only become experience-able in a particular way when an actor conducts practical action toward them. Mead (1932a) described the constitution of objects through practical action by citing the example of a book that lies on a table. He argued that the properties of the book are progressively experienced as the actor notices the object, walks towards it, reaches for it, and grasps the book in a particular way. In this sense, action and experience are in a reflexive relationship. How an object is experienced is not defined by its intrinsic properties or by an individual's cognitive processes. Instead particular aspects of an object are noticed and experienced when, through the course of practical action, a myriad other possibilities for action that would constitute the object in other ways are progressively eliminated; action and experience are merged into one and are inseparable, and each action-experience is based on a prior action-experience, and forms the basis for a next action-experience reflexively constituting the world moment-by-moment (Mead 1932b).

Many actions through which people experience the world are based on habits that are undertaken without 'following' instructions quasi independently until they meet an obstacle or resistance that raises doubt on the usual procedure. Such doubt encourages reflection about the situation and leads to creative efforts to come to a solution and produce the next action in the process. Emirbayer and Maynard (2011: 228) therefore suggested that in the pragmatist's view, "[t]hinking is what occurs most especially in situations where regular channels of action no longer suffice, where conflicts or ruptures in practice cause perplexity." From a pragmatic perspective, "thinking," therefore, is a practice that people rely on when they encounter difficulties continuing with their actions in the usual way. While pragmatists like James, Peirce, and Dewey were primarily interested in further developing theories of thinking and intelligence, the social worker Jane Addams used the pragmatist perspective on action and experience to practically intervene in people's lives. At the end of the nineteenth century, Addams conducted ethnographies of situations where actors faced practical problems and, for a moment, were rendered helpless and perplexed. For example, personnel of a charity recruited mainly from the middle classes were often perplexed and helpless when, in the course of their work, they first encountered the misery and distress among the poor in Chicago. The result was a situational "crisis" that required these personnel to conduct action to normalize the situation (Addams 1912; Emirbayer and Maynard 2011).

This brings us to another point of connection between pragmatism and ethnomethodology, namely *language* and *interaction*. When confronted with practical problems, actors do not think about the situation, rather they engage in talk and interaction with others to deal with the situation. Pragmatists, in particular Peirce and Dewey, created the concept of a tri-partite relationship between symbols, language, and recipient, and argued that the meaning of language relied on actors vocalizing and gesturing, and recipients interpreting. Language, therefore, was not an abstract system of signs and symbols, but a means that actors used to reflect on problematic circumstances and to restore order by using symbols, and language in discourse with each other (Emirbayer and Maynard 2011).

George Herbert Mead expanded these concepts of language and the three-partite relationship between symbols, language, and recipient, and in doing so, developed a concept of communication (Mead 1926). In his view, the meaning of an action produced by actor A arises in and through the response of actor B. For *intersubjectivity* to emerge, therefore, the trajectories of actions produced by different actors need to arrive at identical attributions of meaning. On the one hand, actors adopt different perspectives of a situation; on the other hand, they are able to communicate with each other and thus align and objectify their perspectives. Thereby, they deploy symbols whose meanings are shared within a given *universe of discourse*.

Blumer (1969) further advanced Mead's theory of communication and concept of interaction to develop a distinct sub-discipline of sociology that nowadays is known as *symbolic interactionism*. Blumer's development of symbolic interactionism, however, increasingly moved away from its pragmatist roots as he conceived of 'the perspective of the actors' as being lodged within their heads. Intersubjectivity thus becomes a construct in the actors' imagination. By "taking the role of the other" and exchanging perspectives, actors are able to generate shared ways of looking at situations.

Garfinkel (2006 [1948]) criticized pragmatism as developed by Blumer and others for having a cognitive bias not present in Mead's (1932b) lectures *Philosophy of the Present*. In *Seeing Sociologically*, Garfinkel (2006 [1948]) agreed with Mead and the pragmatists' reflexive linkage of action and experience. However, he distanced his work from the cognitive concept of intersubjectivity implied in much of interactionism and suggested that the pragmatists, unfortunately, had focused on the individual actor and neglected to explain the possibility of social order. Already in *Seeing Sociologically*, Garfinkel wished to provide the basis for a sociological perspective that allowed a shift in orientation to social order and intersubjectivity which prioritized practical action. In his view, intersubjectivity, i.e., the social order of action, was not lodged in people's heads, but could be observed, experienced, and understood through people's practices.

While this explanation of the diverging views on intersubjectivity taken by ethnomethodology and symbolic interactionism clarify that they offer two very different sociological perspectives, sociological textbooks often discuss Garfinkel and ethnomethodology in conjunction with Mead, Blumer, and symbolic interactionism, as Rawls (2002) critically noted. Moreover, various attempts have been made, often initiated by interactionists, to compare ethnomethodology and interactionism. Denzin (1969), for example, elaborated on the commonalities between the two perspectives and eventually tried to show how and why interactionism provided a better solution to sociological questions than ethnomethodology.

These attempts have been seen as undermining the opportunities offered by ethnomethodology and therefore have been strongly countered by Rawls and others (Boden 1990a&b; Gallant and Kleinman 1983, 1985; Hardesty 1982; Rawls 1985, 1989a), who have emphasized that comparisons between these two perspectives begin from the wrong proposition because the ethnomethodological way to explore and analyze social situations fundamentally differs from that of interactionists. Ethnomethodologists shift the focus from the individual actor and her/his plans and motives (Blum and McHugh 1971; Sharrock and Watson 1984) – that interactionists lodge in people's heads – to the practical action of participants in social situations. In their view, social order is not based on cognitive processes, motives, attentions, plans, and projects; rather, plans and motives only come into being in and through the accomplishment of actions. Only in hindsight, when the events are reconsidered post-hoc does it becomes possible to refer to motives and plans to explain the organization of a situation.

## The *Interaction Order:* Goffman and Garfinkel

Like Garfinkel and ethnomethodology, sociological textbooks also discuss Erving Goffman's work as a version of symbolic interactionism. Goffman knew Mead's work very well and was in close contact with Herbert Blumer, who was dean at Berkeley when Goffman took up a position as Assistant Professor in 1959. Goffman did not regard himself as an interactionist, but considered the use of the denotation *symbolic interactionism* itself as an attempt by Chicago's sociologists to differentiate themselves from other sociologists, and he opposed this fragmentation of sociology (Raab 2008; Smith 2006).

Goffman's intellectual link to symbolic interactionism stemmed from his concern with the analysis of identity and the constitution and management of identity in social interaction. In his most famous book, *The Presentation of Self in Everyday Life* (Goffman 1990 [1959]), he began to develop methods and concepts to analyze and describe the interaction order through which identity is created and maintained. Goffman continued this program of research by investigating the interaction order he observed in casinos, at parties, or in other public places.

From the start Garfinkel resisted accepting Goffman's drive to develop concepts, models and types to describe social situations. As Rawls (2006) explains in her introduction to *Seeing Sociologically,* Goffman had encouraged Garfinkel to publish his 1948 manuscript. It may have been this encouragement by a sociologist who had an interest in the development of theoretical concepts that made Garfinkel doubt the value of his book up until 2006; in Garfinkel's view, the concepts, types, and models that were at the center of *Seeing Sociologically* were inadequate means to describe *social order.*

Despite these differences, Garfinkel and Goffman shared the view that, unfortunately, contemporary sociology neglected to analyze the order of the everyday (Goffman 1972, 1983; Rawls 1987, 2003b). Goffman, however, stuck to his position that sociology needed to develop concepts, schemes, and types in its description of society. His sociology seemed closely tied to Schutz's view, insofar as it implied that actors make sense of social situations and events by using concepts and typologies to interpret them (Smith 2006).

Garfinkel was critical of sociological approaches that relied on the assumption that participants deployed types and schemes when they acted and interacted in social situations. As Hutchinson and colleagues (Hutchinson, Read, and Sharrock 2008: 104) suggested, "Goffman's [sociology] does not enable us to understand an activity, which really puzzles us, but seeks to relate those actions which do not (from the point of view of their intelligibility) puzzle us to themes and preoccupations of his professional colleagues."

Garfinkel distanced his sociology from Goffman's by focusing on the observable-and-reportable practices through which social order is ongoing and concretely produced, moment-by-moment. His principal concern was with the details of social action and its organization. Garfinkel's analyses explored the indexicality of action and their contingent accomplishment in complex situations, in order to explicate the methods that participants use to produce social order. His prime concern is with the constitutive practice of social order, while Goffman, in contrast, contested the possibility that sociology was able to investigate and elaborate on the constitutive *basic rules* or *methods* of social action (Raab 2008).

## Ethnomethodology and Conversation Analysis

Garfinkel and Goffman's different understandings of *social order* may have been one of the reasons why Goffman's doctoral student, Harvey Sacks (1935–1975), joined Garfinkel at UC Los Angeles. According to Schegloff (1992), Sacks had studied for a Bachelor of Arts (BA) at Columbia College (1955) and then a Bachelor of Laws (LLB) at Yale (1959), where he regularly attended seminars by Harold Lasswell and developed an interest in sociological questions such as how the law as an institution worked. Subsequently, Sacks enrolled as a graduate student in Political Science at MIT in Cambridge, Massachusetts; he attended lectures by Noam Chomsky who, at the time, was interested in the structure of language, and seminars by Talcott Parsons. At one of Parsons' seminars he met Garfinkel, who was spending his sabbatical leave from UCLA at Harvard. The two quickly discovered a shared enthusiasm for the study of natural interaction and social order.

When it became clear to Sacks that he would not be able to pursue his interests fully in Cambridge, he left MIT and, in the academic year 1959/60, followed the advice of Harold Lasswell to study for a degree at UC Berkeley. This California university appealed to him as he was able to study with Philip Selznick, who had a particular interest in organizations, bureaucracy, and legal institutions; withHerbert Blumer; and then, in 1960, with Erving Goffman (Schegloff 1989). At Berkeley, Sacks had a number of colleagues who shared his interest in studying naturally occurring social interaction and who later became key figures in the development of ethnomethodology and conversation analysis; they included Roy Turner, Emanuel Schegloff, David Sudnow, and others. As part of his doctoral research, Sacks examined audio-recordings of telephone calls at a Suicide Prevention Center in Los Angeles. For the purpose of the analysis, Sacks moved from Berkeley to Los Angeles in 1963, which encouraged his close collaboration with Garfinkel (Smith

2006). Both shared with Goffman an interest in naturalistic data, but while Goffman largely relied on ethnographic observations, Sacks and Garfinkel became increasingly interested in the detailed analysis of recorded talk. Through their examination of telephone calls they strove to reveal the social organization of talk.

Sacks' shift of interest toward studies of the fine detailed analysis of talk became a problem for his PhD studies at Berkeley. Goffman considered Sacks' analysis as circular and irrelevant. Only when Aaron Cicourel stepped in as chair of the examination committee was Sacks able to complete his PhD at Berkeley (Raab 2008). Although Sacks left Goffman, it is clear that he remained one of the key influences on Sacks' work, although there are only few mentions of Goffman in his lectures (Sacks 1992). Future studies of Sacks' work may reveal Goffman's influence on conversation analysis.

By examining naturally occurring talk rather than artificially generated talk sequences, Sacks' research showed a relationship to Simmel's sociology and his development of social forms. Sacks' studies fundamentally differed from contemporary social scientific research concerned with the structure of talk, such as Chomsky's analyses, as well as from the research undertaken by Robert Freed Bales (1976 [1950]) and George Caspar Homans (1961), because they were designed to reveal the base elements of interaction (cf. Silverman 1998).

By scrutinizing short sequences of talk, Sacks was not interested in reconstructing how one utterance follows a prior one; rather, his concern lay with understanding the interactional context of utterances (Sacks 1992, Schegloff 1992). In his view, the meaning of an action, such as a single utterance or a gesture, was not lodged in actors' heads, but in the action itself. It therefore could not be retrieved by interviewing the actors; instead it required a detailed analysis of the sequential production of action. He argued that each action is produced in light of a prior one and provides the framework for each subsequent action (cf. Heritage 1984: 242). Conversation analysis inspects the moment of the production of an action and asks why this action has been produced now and in this particular way. Sacks' analyses were strongly influenced by Garfinkel's development of ethnomethodology, as he explained in his paper on "Sociological description" (Sacks 1963). The concept of *sequence* and of the *sequential organization* of action could already be found in Garfinkel's 1948 manuscript (Rawls 2006: 29–41), which Sacks may well have known about. Despite this close connection between ethnomethodology and conversation analysis, however, conversation analysis runs the risk that the researcher may forget the ethnomethodological pursuit of people's deployment of *folk methods* to constitute social order and instead deploy a mere technical analysis of conversation. Indeed, nowadays, it can be observed that linguistics has adopted conversation analysis for its own purposes, with little interest in sociological questions, while sociologists have long neglected Garfinkel's and Sacks' interest in the detailed organization of action and the constitution of social order.[2]

Fairly recently, video-based studies of interaction have taken up Garfinkel and Sacks' original sociological interests to pursue the exploration of the interactional organization of work. A growing body of research concerned with workplace studies of interaction in cars and public places uses the newly developed concept of *multimodality* to conduct sequential analysis of oral, visible, and material action based on scrutiny of video-recordings (Engestrom and Middleton 1998; Heath and Luff 2000; Llewellyn and Hindmarsh 2010; Luff, Hindmarsh, and Heath 2000; Pinch and Clark 1986; Goodwin and Goodwin 1996). These developments have reinvigorated a wider interest in ethnomethodology and conversation analysis that we return to in the next chapter.

## Ethnomethodology and Phenomenological Sociology

Due to Garfinkel's strong interest in Schutz's phenomenology, ethnomethodology is also often discussed together with phenomenological sociology (Douglas 1974; Rogers 1983). Indeed, some textbooks describe ethnomethodology as a sociology that fundamentally relies on phenomenology and primarily deploys a subjectivist perspective. The previous chapters have refuted this view and have demonstrated that in his theoretical work in the 1940s and 1950s, Garfinkel was already pursuing an interest in the social organization of action.

However, it cannot be ignored that when he was studying for his master's degree in Newark, Garfinkel intensely examined the phenomenological writings of Husserl and Schutz. Garfinkel's references to Merleau-Ponty in later writings suggested that he remained interested in phenomenology throughout his academic career. In *Seeing Sociologically* (2006 [1948]), as well as in his doctoral thesis (1952), Garfinkel discussed Schutz's concept of the everyday. While Schutz, and later phenomenological social theory, was primarily concerned with interpreting the everyday from the perspective of the actor, Garfinkel preferred Talcott Parsons' concern for the social organization of action in the everyday. In his early writings, Garfinkel combined Parsons' concerns with the characteristics of the everyday that Schutz has elaborated on in his writings. Thus, Garfinkel came to develop *accounts*, i.e., "observable-and-reportable" action, as the foundation of social order, as they allowed participants to align with each other's action. The focus of his research, therefore, lay with the *efforts* that actors put into the production of communicative means to accomplish intersubjectivity in social situations (Garfinkel 2006 [1948]). For the purpose of his analysis, Garfinkel replaced the imaginary perspective of the actor, which was the starting point for analyses in phenomenological sociology and symbolic interactionism, with the perspective of how social order arises from actors' making "observable-and-reportable" the organization of their action. His focus, therefore, was on locally observable and intelligible sequences of action.

As Garfinkel continued to elaborate his program of research and developed an interest in *Studies of Work* (1986), he turned his focus to the examination of *embodied practices* (Garfinkel 2002). This interest in practice was influenced by the phenomenological distinction between Body and Lived-Body, i.e., the biological body and the body that acts and experiences the world, that points toward the embodied character of experiences and the visibility of practice, allowing participants to make social order an accountable accomplishment (Eberle and Maeder 2011; Eberle 2012). Within ethnomethodological studies of work there are studies that pursue a strong interest in the phenomenological interpretation of activities. They highlight the principle of unique adequacy of descriptions and are undertaken by ethnomethodologists who have acquired the competences of professionals, such as mathematicians (Livingston), jazz musicians (Sudnow), and lawyers (Burns).

Despite attempts to marginalize ethnomethodology within sociology, over the past decades it has retained a firm place in sociology, which is evidenced by its presence in sociological textbooks; faculty positions at universities around the world; and the large attendance at conferences held by international associations such as the Ethnomethodology and Conversational Analysis (EMCA) Section of the American Sociological Association and the International Institute of Ethnomethodology and Conversation Analysis (IIEMCA). Moreover, ethnomethodological research has had an important influence on debates of sociological theory, research, and methods, which I discuss in the following chapter.

# Chapter 9

# Ethnomethodology's Influence on Recent Developments in Sociology

It is quite surprising that despite its fifty-year history, sociological textbooks still primarily see ethnomethodology as being concerned with breaching experiments and conversation analysis (cf. Appelrouth and Edles 2008). They also discuss it together with phenomenological sociology, symbolic interactionism, and cognate micro-theories of action, already strongly criticized by Garfinkel in his early work. By linking ethnomethodology to other theories of action and micro-sociology and by focusing on the breaching experiments and conversation analysis, these textbooks ignore not only Garfinkel's position in relation to those sociological traditions, but also the varieties of ethnomethodology that have developed since the 1960s (Maynard and Clayman 1991). They also neglect to take into consideration the influence of ethnomethodology on other disciplines and areas of research. Some of these areas are briefly covered in this chapter.

## Ethnomethodology and Sociological Theory

Over the past few years, attempts have been made, mainly but not exclusively in German sociology, to link conversation analysis to *systems theory* as developed by Niklas Luhmann (1996). Luhmann has rejuvenated Parsons' functionalist theory by drawing on developments in biology, and analyzes society as an "autopoietic" and "self-referential" communication system. In this view, society is an ongoing process made up of communication that is sequentially organized. Luhmann's theory is highly abstract and not concerned with the organization of practical communication within society or its subsystems of science,

*Harold Garfinkel: The Creation and Development of Ethnomethodology* by Dirk vom Lehn. 147–167. © 2013 UVK Verlagsgesellschaft mbH; additional material for English edition © 2014 Left Coast Press, Inc. All rights reserved.

art, education, economy, politics, etc. People have no place in this theory and systems independently continue with their communication, moment-by-moment. This very brief characterization of systems theory reflects some of the possible links between Luhmann's theory and conversation analysis, such as the sequential organization of communication and the importance of temporality in the process of communication, that are also of such importance in Garfinkel and Sacks' writing. One of Luhmann's starting points is Parsons' functionalist paradigm. Yet unlike Parsons, Luhmann, like Garfinkel and Sacks, is concerned with the fleetingness, rather than the presumed stability of social order and meaning (Luhmann 1996). In light of these seemingly interesting points of connection, Hausendorf (2004) and Schneider (2000), as well as more recently Liu (2012), argue that sequences of interaction could be conceived and analyzed as processes through which social order, or in Luhmann's sense *systems* ,are produced.

Yet it remains unclear whether either conversation analysis or systems theory gains from such an approach to studying social action. Systems theory remains on a very abstract level, while conversation analysis is concerned with participants' accomplishment of action. Even when scholars like Kieserling (1999), who wrote a fascinating book on communication among co-present participants from a systems theory perspective, turn their interest to interaction, we fail to learn much new about it. Such scholars make important contributions to system theory thinking, but do not add much to studies of interaction (Knoblauch 2000).

The argument that there is no fruitful relationship between systems theory and ethnomethodology or conversation analysis may be seen as another justification for the irrelevance of ethnomethodology to debates in sociological and social theory. Yet as I have variously highlighted in this book, ethnomethodology orients to theory in a very different way from sociological theory (Helm 1989; Rawls 1987; Wilson and Zimmerman 1979). This also becomes apparent in David Bogen's (1999) critical investigation of Habermas' (1987) theory of communicative action, which elaborates on how ethnomethodological inquiries, with their focus on practice, can be used to rethink the linguistic basis of Habermas' theory. In fact, he argues that Habermas' theory of communicative action is, so far at least, too removed from communicative practice as it has failed to engage with the large body of empirical studies of the social order.

These points of contact between ethnomethodology and sociological theory make clear the interest ethnomethodologists have (and always have had) in engaging with questions of sociological theory, although they may have approached sociological theory in ways that some might consider unconventional. In this chapter I refer to *praxis theory* to further elaborate on the important contributions that Garfinkel, and therewith ethnomethodology, has made to contemporary theoretical discussions in sociology. Subsequently, I briefly discuss Garfinkel's influence on developments in sociological subfields: social problems, gender studies, organization studies, educational research, and studies of behavior in public places.

## Ethnomethodology and Praxis Theory

In the previous chapters I have repeatedly referred to Garfinkel's view on the relationship between ethnomethodology and developments in sociological theory. I noted that one of the major contributions of ethnomethodology to sociological theory and research is its interest in the contingent details of action that are ignored by traditional, formal-analytic sociology with its concern for objectivity and generalizability. Recent debates about praxis theory illustrate ethnomethodology's contribution.

In *Seeing Sociologically* (2006 [1948]), Garfinkel suggested that by the 1940s, when he was studying Husserl and Schutz, he had already begun to develop an interest in practice and the practical accomplishment of action. In light of his reading of phenomenology, Garfinkel concerned himself with examining how everyday categories, or *typifications*, as Schutz (Kim and Berard 2009; Psathas 1999; Schutz 1967a) called them, are produced through practice. While other sociological perspectives often lodged such typifications and sense-making processes inside people's heads, Garfinkel was interested in their embodied and practical instantiation.

The transformation of mental or cognitive categories into embodied practices provides a pertinent link between ethnomethodology and recent attempts to develop a theory of practice. Over the past few years, Theodore Schatzki and others (Schatzki, Knorr-Cetina, and Savigny 2000) have begun to explain the importance of a theory of practice for sociological theory. In their recent edited volume, Schatzki and colleagues criticize previous theories of practice, such as those developed by Bourdieu (1977) and Giddens (1986), because both, in different ways, referred to Garfinkel and ethnomethodology. Bourdieu (1977) characterized Garfinkel as an interactionist and ethnomethodology as reductionist because, in his view, it was unable to explain the relationship between practice and structure. Giddens (1986), by contrast, used Garfinkel's studies to explain the link between actor and structure, by referring to the importance of routinized practices for social order.

In these debates about theories of practice, we can therefore see how ethnomethodology has been examined in terms of its relevance to address the question of the link between micro and macro that has troubled sociology since its origins. Some ethnomethodologists have addressed this by respecifying the question and characterizing the distinction between micro and macro as a conceptual distinction that can only become (seen as) relevant as far as actors in concrete situations orient to it (Coulter 2000; Lynch 2000b; Berard 2005). Current debates about practice and theory of practice argue that routinized aspects of practical action that include oral and bodily action as well as the use of instruments provide accounts for structure.

## Ethnomethodology and Social Problems

Ethnomethodology has often been criticized and considered irrelevant to the big sociological debates and to questions of importance to society (Coser 1975; Gellner 1975). This criticism is without foundation.

From the outset of his studies of sociology, Garfinkel himself had a strong interest in matters of inequality and race. This interest is apparent in his 1940 short story "Color Trouble" and in his master's degree research, which was later published in *Social Forces* (1949), the journal that Howard Odum established as an outlet concerned with research on social issues such as inequality, racial segregation, and poverty. Aside from Garfinkel's early research, a substantial body of ethnomethodological research has emerged that studies a wide range of social problems. While the collection *Understanding Social Problems* edited by Zimmerman, Wieder, and Zimmerman (1976) is not solely devoted to the ethnomethodological concern with poverty, race, sexism, inequality, social justice, etc., the fact that it was collated by major figures in ethnomethodology indicates the commitment of these scholars to the study of social problems. It is therefore not surprising that in 1988 Douglas Maynard published a Special Issue of the journal *Social Problems* titled "Language, Social Interaction, and Social Problems."

Such ethnomethodological studies of social problems emerged against the background of a burgeoning field of sociological research on social problems (cf. Clarke 2001) that, from an ethnomethodological point of view, failed to capture the practices that produce social problems and generate "problematic people" and "problematic actions." Ethnomethodologists asked, "Do we need a general theory of social problems?" (Bogen and Lynch 2007) and since the 1960s have conducted a wide range of studies that reveal how, in different circumstances, including institutional contexts such as courts, prisons, and police departments, people are categorized as delinquent because their actions are treated as misaligned with the accepted moral and normative order.

One such moral and normative order is "the convict code" that Lawrence Wieder (1974) investigated in his doctoral dissertation. His research elaborated on how this code of conduct is not a theoretical concept, but a practical achievement by the inmates and personnel in a halfway house for paroled narcotic addicts. In a related way, another doctoral student of Garfinkel's, Egon Bittner, has produced an extensive body of studies that explores the relationship between rules in books and rules in practice (cf. Carlin and Slack 2013). His studies focus on the work of the police and the ways in which participants acquire the competences and skills of policemen. As part of his research he famously investigated the practices deployed by patrolmen to keep the peace in skid row[1] and skid row–like districts. He differentiated these practices from those that patrolmen produce to enforce the law in other areas. This differentiation is based on the patrolmen's orientation to the situation they encounter in such troubled urban areas where they feel they have a "mandate" to deal with certain issues, by coercion if need be (Bittner 1967; Silbey and Bittner 1982). Policemen's ability to differentiate between situations of law enforcement relies on the acquisition of competences that allows them to handle "a multitude of what seem like unique situations over and over again" (Bayley and Bittner 1984: 35).

Bittner's and Wieder's studies on the situated and interpretive practice and procedures that participants deploy to identify and deal with social problems have provided the basis for much of the recent research concerned with deviance, discrimination, and crime (Berard 2010, 2012); police work and the social construction of social problems (Ibarra and Kitsuse 1997); and recent developments in interactionist studies of social problems (Holstein and Miller 1993).

Alongside these ethnomethodological studies of social problems, a large body of ethnomethodological studies has emerged that explores the organization of courtroom procedures and "law in action" (Travers and Manzo 1997) more generally. This strand of ethnomethodological research has become very influential in the sociology of law (cf. Burns 1997, 2001; Dingwall 2000; Mair, Watson, Elsey, and Smith 2012; Peyrot and Burns 2001; Travers 1997). Ethnomethodological interest in courtroom procedures remains strong, evidenced by the recent publication of Baudouin Dupret's *Adjudication in Action* (2012; Jenkings 2013), a detailed study of procedures in an Egyptian court. In this research, the ethnomethodological interest in the relationship between practice and order that is so vividly embodied in courtroom procedures continues.

## Ethnomethodology and Gender Studies

Garfinkel's study of the transgendered Agnes, published in *Studies* (Garfinkel 1967g, k) has become a cornerstone for the emergence of Gender Studies, where it is now regarded as one of its classic texts. In this study, Garfinkel explored the practical efforts of the transsexual to "pass" as a woman in social situations. In Western societies, the distinction between conventional male and female as gender roles remained unquestioned until the 1960s. Garfinkel's study of Agnes shed doubt on this distinction and demonstrated that gender is not a stable property a person owns, but is a practical achievement that people produce moment-by-moment through their action.

Garfinkel (1967g: 118) argued that *gender* is an aspect of social interaction that is "omnirelevant." In social situations, participants mutually attribute each other with a particular gender and, based on this attribution, expect the other to act in a certain way. If participants were to suddenly change their gender within an ongoing situation, this would be perceived as an *accountable* incongruency; we can sometimes observe such spontaneous changes of gender identity in a playful manner at parties. When a person wishes to change her/his gender in the everyday, it is therefore necessary to produce actions that are recognizable as the actions of a particular gender. This observation led Garfinkel to the conclusion that Agnes, despite having male genitals, manages to pass as a woman because she is a *practical methodologist* who in an ongoing and practical fashion produces accounts of how she deploys her everyday knowledge and competences to make her actions "observable-and-reportable" as gender-specific practices.

Following Garfinkel's analysis and in the context of the emergence of conversation analysis, a body of literature has been produced that is primarily concerned with the relationship between gender and social interaction. For example, studies have explored how participants constitute gender as a relevant category in interaction, involving analyses that, within conversation analysis, are often discussed in the context of "membership categorization analysis" (Stokoe 2010; Schegloff 2007b).

The ethnomethodological perspective, therefore, stands in contrast to arguments that suggest that people of different genders deploy different interactional styles. Instead, conversation analysis investigates phenomena such as the discrimination against women in everyday conversations by revealing, for example, the distribution of turns at talk and the interruption of talk (Kitzinger 2000; Speer and Stokoe 2011; Stokoe 2000, 2003, 2006, 2010).

Nowadays gender studies is such a widely accepted area of research that the significance of Garfinkel's analysis and its contribution to the field is sometimes forgotten. Well-known research, such as studies by Kessler and McKenna (1985) or Hirschauer (1998), however, refers to Garfinkel's argument for the ongoing production of gender, or, as they now call it, "doing gender" (Ayass 2007; West and Zimmerman 1987, 2009). Although gender research nowadays includes a multitude of theories and approaches, ethnomethodology and conversation analysis still make important contributions to this area.

## Workplace Studies and Organization Studies

A few decades ago, David Silverman (1970) observed that he was surprised that ethnomethodology was not more influential in organization studies. It took until the 1980s before organizational theory and related research discovered ethnomethodology, and its influence has subsequently increased. Since then, a large number of ethnographic studies have been conducted that have drawn on, or at least referred to, Garfinkel's ethnomethodological program. These studies have taken up Garfinkel's explanation of the *shop floor* problem and have begun to investigate the organization of work in factories, air traffic control, hospitals, and elsewhere (Boden 1994; Button 1993; Button and Sharrock 2002, 2009; Crabtree 2001, 2003; Harper 1997; Hughes 2001; Rouncefield and Tolmie 2011).

At the center of these studies is not the organization itself, but the process of organizing, as Garfinkel and other ethnomethodologists had argued since the 1960s (Bittner 1965; Garfinkel 1956b, 2002).

Their aim is to analyze and describe work practices in such a way that their description can inform the development and deployment of new technologies and practice. In so doing they are continuing Garfinkel's (2002) *hybrid studies of work* program that rests upon an intertwining of ethnomethodological studies and actual work practice.

Ethnomethodological ethnographies of work have commonalities with a related strand of research, namely video-based studies of work that highlight the importance of the smallest details of action for the organization of work. Charles Goodwin (1981) and Christian Heath (1986) are widely seen as pioneers of this strand of ethnomethodological research, which has a close relationship to conversation analysis and its interest in the organization of talk in institutional settings (Drew and Heritage 1992). These video-based studies of work use analytic and methodological tools such as transcripts developed in conversation analysis to investigate how participants organize their oral, visible, and material or material actions. Of particular interest is the interweaving of the material environment with participants' practices.[2]

Examples of such studies that have been conducted include those undertaken at the Work, Interaction and Technology Research Centre at King's College London, examining the practices of managers and personnel involved in activities in technology-rich settings such as control-rooms of urban transport systems and newsrooms; the cooperation of nurses and anesthetists in operating theaters and other health care and health service settings, including dentistry and optometry; the work of designers in architecture; and the navigation and exploration of museums (Heath 2012; Heath and Luff 2000; Heath, Knoblauch and Luff 2000; Hindmarsh and Heath 2000; Hindmarsh 2010; Luff, Heath, and Pitsch 2009; vom Lehn, Heath, and Hindmarsh 2001). These projects have examined in detail how participants interweave their action with features of the visual and material environment through the organization of their practices.

The research undertaken at the Work, Interaction and Technology Research Centre and at universities in Europe, the USA, and Japan, as well as conducted at commercial research institutes such as

PARC in Palo Alto (California), IBM, and at the Microsoft Research Labs in Cambridge (UK) and Grenoble (Switzerland) have led to the emergence of a distinct area of research called *workplace studies*. Since the 1990s, workplace studies have contributed to debates about technological innovation and design as well as the organization of work. These research teams explore the interweaving of complex technologies with interaction and the organization of work (Henderson, Whalen, and Whalen 2002; Moore, Whalen, and Hankinson 2010; Moore 2012; Suchman 1996, 2006; Szymanski and Whalen 2011; Vinkhuyzen and Whalen 2000; Vinkhuyzen et al. 2006; Whalen, et al. 2004; Whalen and Zimmerman 2005).

Furthermore, there are a number of small research teams that use video recording as principal data to explore the organization of work practices. The best-known of these teams is probably the cooperation between Charles and Marjorie Goodwin who, since the 1980s, have been leading the development of video-based studies of interaction. Over the past few decades, the Goodwins have analyzed the organization of the work of airport personnel and girls in schools (Goodwin and Goodwin 1996; Goodwin 2006). Charles Goodwin has also analyzed situations where one of the participants, due to a stroke, had difficulties in orally and visibly communicating in the same way as his co-participants. In these studies Goodwin focused on revealing the methods and techniques that participants use in such situations to establish, if only momentarily, intersubjectivity (Goodwin 2006; McNeill and Goodwin 2000). In other studies he has examined how archaeologists deploy standardized charts to constitute color and categorize material (Goodwin 1997; Goodwin 2000).

Video-based studies of interaction have also found an audience within management and organization studies. Since the 1970s these areas of study have seen a rise in "critical" perspectives on management that have a particular interest in the details of the organization of work. Research in these areas has, therefore, increasingly used qualitative methods such as discourse analysis and ethnography, and, more recently, has begun to explore the opportunities offered by ethnomethodology, conversation analysis, and video-based studies of work practice (Llewellyn 2008; Llewellyn and Hindmarsh 2010; Samra-Fredericks 2004; Samra-Fredericks and Bargiela-Chiappini 2008).

Although I have largely discussed workplace studies as an area of studies related to ethnomethodology, they really encapsulate a much larger theoretical and methodological scope. In particular, they also include *activity theory* and *distributed cognition*, which use ethnography and video analysis for their studies. The inclusion of multiple conceptual approaches into its scope has helped workplace studies to widen its influence on a broad range of disciplines, including sociology, psychology, and the cognitive sciences, as well as studies of work and organization (Engestrom and Middleton 1998). This influence has also stretched into the technical sciences, such as Computer-Supported Cooperative Work (CSCW) and Human-Computer Interaction (HCI), where the hybridization of research and practice has led to the use of ethnographies to inform the design of new technologies (Hughes et al. 1994; Martin, Mariani, and Rouncefield 2007; O'Malley et al. 2006; Randall, Shapiro, and Hughes 1992; Randall, Marr, and Rouncefield 2001).

## Interaction in Health and Medical Situations

Related to the body of studies concerned with talk and interaction in institutional settings (Drew and Heritage 1992; Heritage and Clayman 2010), one of the most active and influential areas within ethnomethodology and conversation analysis to emerge investigates interaction between patients, medical practitioners, and health care providers. Here, the main corpus of studies is concerned with general practice where, first, conversation analysts and video analysts explored the organization of talk and interaction between doctor and patient (Heath 1986; Heritage and Maynard 2006; Sarangi and Roberts 1999).

Frankel's (1984) study, which explores how routine sequences between doctor and patient arise in light of the contingencies involved in these encounters is sometimes seen as one of the pioneering studies in this area (Maynard and Heritage 2005). He found that microanalysis of interaction, i.e., conversation analysis, allowed the researcher access to the ways in which doctor and patient orient to each other's actions. From here on a wide range of studies emerged that explained the organization of opening and closing of medical consultations; the organization of participation in consultations; the display of pain; explanations given for treatments; and the delivery of good and bad news, etc. (Heath 1982, 1989; Heritage and Stivers 1999; Mangione-Smith, Stivers and Elliott 2003).

A related body of studies has emerged that explores the organization of interaction in health care and health service domains. Peräkylä and colleagues (2008) use conversation analysis for the study of the organization of psychotherapy consultations. This has led to investigations of how medical experts, i.e., psychotherapists, gain access to the goings-on in patients' brains. These studies allow access to professional practice designed to provide accounts for psychological states and processes. Hence, Peräkylä and Vehviläinen (2003) have explored what professional knowledge psychotherapists deploy to find out about the cognitive processes of their patients. McCabe and colleagues (2002) have also investigated interaction in psychotherapy consultations. Their focus, however, has been the difficulty faced by psychotherapists and the practical solutions they use to manage patients' participations in the interaction. Other health care and health service areas under investigation include been teamwork in anesthesia (Hindmarsh and Pilnick 2007); the organization of communication in physiotherapy (Parry 2006, 2013); the work of dentists (Hindmarsh 2010); consultations in obesity clinics (Webb 2009); and the ways in which optometrists organize consultations in optometry and assess their clients' eyesight (vom Lehn et al. 2012; Webb, Heath, vom Lehn, and Gibson 2013).

Ethnomethodological, conversation analytic, and video-based studies of medical interaction and interaction in health care domains are a burgeoning field of research that, aside from their contribution to academic debates about health and medicine, cognition, intersubjectivity of perception, and related areas, have also made some interesting contributions to practice. Anssi Peräkyläs work on psychotherapy is very good example in this regard, but there is a wide range of further contributions to practice, in particular on the communication practice of health care and general practitioners (Antaki 2011).

## Child Development and Educational Research

Following Garfinkel's concern with the *respecification* of taken-for-granted phenomena as "locally produced, naturally accountable phenomena of order" (Garfinkel 2002: 118, Fn. 45), various ethno-methodologists have become interested in revealing the mundane practices through which scientific concepts, theories, and ideas are produced. One such theory that pervades not only the cognitive sciences and psychology, but also many everyday interactions, is the concept of cognition, the mind, and intelligence. In particular, Jeff Coulter (1983, 1989; Coulter and Watson 2008) has respecified the concepts and theories underlying *cognitivism* and the taken-for-grantedness of "mind" as "something" lodged in people's heads. His prolific writings have provided the theoretical basis for ethnomethodological and cognate research in areas like the sociology of emotions, and to debates and controversies about the uses of Wittgenstein's thinking when respecifying "cognition" and "the mind" and when considering references to motives and modes of perception in studies of interaction (McHoul and Rapley 2001; Sharrock and Coulter 1998).

Aside from these theoretical developments in ethnomethodology concerned with cognition and the mind, it was Anthony Wootton (2005) who began to study, in detail, interaction between adults and young children, and to explore learning as an interactional achievement. His research is concerned with how learning requires interactional competence that children acquire from a very young age as they grow up. He positions his studies alongside the growing interest in Vygotskyian theories of the mind, the arguments in the learning sciences that social interaction is important for cognitive development (Vygotsky and Cole 1978; Wertsch 1991). Through his studies of parent–child conversations,

Wootton (2006) shows that in everyday situations the origin of children's actions is often ascribed to their mental capabilities. This ascription to the child's mind, however, is not unavoidable, as their competencies can just as well be seen as practical abilities they bring to bear in interaction. For example, as Wootton (2005) explains, in the course of their upbringing children progressively acquire competencies to position requests and other actions in sequential places that are more likely to elicit required responses.

Wootton's important contribution to ethnomethodological research on cognitive development can be seen in relationship to a body of work that explores the organization of interaction and talk in educational settings such as schools. One of the earliest ethnomethodological studies of an educational setting is Cicourel and Kitsuse's (1963) investigation of the ways in which school counselors make decisions that influence the career of pupils. From here on, a large body of studies concerned with classroom interaction has emerged that explores the organization of talk between teachers and pupils (Hester and Francis 2000).

Mehan's studies (1978, 1979) of the organization of classroom interaction described the three-part structure of sequences produced by teachers and students when examining sequences produced to test students' knowledge or understanding: (1) the "initiation" elicits (2) a reply from the student that engenders (3) an evaluation produced by the teacher. Mehan considered these three parts of the sequences as "two coupled 'adjacency pairs,'" i.e., initiation and reply coupled with reply and evaluation (Mehan 1978, 1979; Macbeth 2003). The body of classroom research that developed within the context of Mehan's studies is sometimes called *constitutive ethnography* (McDermott, Gospodinoff, and Aron 1978). Its innovation lies in the use of audio-/video-recorded "naturalistic" data as principal data to explore how classroom interaction is organized. By using these data, it is possible to examine in detail the "local order" in and through which education and learning take place. For example, related studies by McHoul (2008) have examined the specifics of "repair" in educational interaction and Maynard and Marlaire (1990,

1992) have investigated sequence organization in IQ-tests.

While these studies have largely focused on the organization of talk, McDermott and colleagues (McDermott, Gospodinoff, and Aron 1978) used video data to investigate how classroom participants bodily orient to each other and to the activity in hand. By drawing on Albert Scheflen's (1973, 1974) famous research, they revealed how the context of activities is displayed by the participants' postures; modifications in posture display changes in activity. Their research, therefore, suggested that participants maintain concerted activities by closely coordinating not only their talk, but also their bodily behavior with each other, and use changes in posture to negotiate each other's participation status in an activity.

These studies in schools and other educational settings have illustrated that learning is an interactional achievement. They have respecified the understanding that learning is a cognitive process and have shown how it can be examined with a specific sociological orientation. In light of this research, a wide range of conversation analytic studies have been concerned, for example, with second language acquisition (Mondada and Doehler 2004) and the teaching of mathematics (Greiffenhagen and Sharrock 2008; Greiffenhagen 2008). In recent years, ethnomethodologists and conversation analysts have expanded the scope of their studies to look into the organization of professional training and the increasing importance of technology in the teaching and learning of professional skills and competences. This body of research includes video-based studies of teaching and learning, for example, in operating theaters (Koschmann et al. 2012b; Mondada 2003; Svensson, Luff, and Heath 2009) and dentistry (Hindmarsh, Reynolds, and Dunne 2009), as well as studies in the growing field of computer-supported cooperative learning (Miyahki et al. 2002).

Aside from studies of interaction in formal educational organizations such as schools, educational research has recently become interested in cognitive development and learning in other, non-formal or informal domains. These informal learning settings include, amongst others, kitchens in family homes, museums, and science centers. In the latter, video-based studies of interaction at exhibits have shifted the focus from the cognitive outcome of people's engagement with exhibits, to the organization of their action and interaction underpinning any learning and cognitive development that might emerge in museums. Such studies have explored how people make sense of interactive exhibits in a railway museum (Hemmings et al. 2000; Marr et al. 1997) and how they use the exhibit features and the space around them to display an understanding of exhibits by producing actions that embellish the display of their engagement and experience of the artifacts (Meisner et al. 2007).

## Behavior in Public Places and Mobility

Despite Goffman's (1963, 1971) early studies of behavior in public places, ethnomethodologists have shown only occasional interest in the ways in which people conduct themselves in and navigate public places. There is, of course, Ryave and Schenkein's (1974) study concerned with the artful ways in which people managed to avoid collisions on the busy pavements and crossings of modern streets. And more recently, Lee and Watson (1993) and Garfinkel and Livingston (2003) have explored the organization of "queues" and "locomotion" on streets and public squares. Save for these rare exceptions, however, it has taken until the arrival of modern video equipment to enliven this field of studies.

Since the late 1990s, the analysis of people navigating and interacting in public domains has begun to take shape. There is now a rich body of research concerned with "mobility in interaction" (Haddington, McIlvenny, and Broth 2008; Haddington, Mondada, and Nevile 2013), both on foot and in vehicles. These studies consider the organization of action through which people, often with very little talk, move along a pier step-by-step (Broth and Lundstrom 2013) and how museum visitors move through galleries (vom Lehn 2012, 2013). These studies are beginning to demonstrate that, at least in some circumstances, bodily action, like talk, is sequentially organized. Like Ryave and Schenkein (1974) in their paper, these studies primarily investigate "walking as a situated practice" and add to prior research on this activity its em-beddedness within a material environment. So, for example, vom Lehn (2013) examines how museum visitors glance or look to neighboring exhibits and through a mutual alignment of shifts in bodily and visual orientation constitute "candidate exhibits" they might move to next. In a related way, studies of guided tours have considered the collaborative exploration of exhibitions, gardens, and other public settings by show-ing how guides moment-by-moment constitute tour participants as an audience that orients not only to the guide, but also to the material and visual environment that is subject to her/his actions (Best 2012; De Stefani 2010; Mondada 2009).

Aside from studies that explore how people walk through spaces in interaction with others, there has been a growing interest in inves-tigating how people use technology such as maps, mobile technology, and vehicles while on the move. These studies reveal that maps are not representations of an external world; rather, they are deployed in in-teraction as occasioned resources to move through a space (Liberman 2013). They include ethnomethodological and conversation analytic research into the ways in which participants embed maps and aspects of maps within their talk and interaction. Psathas (1986), for example, reveals how, in talk and interaction, participants turn a map into some-thing useful that helps them to find a "correspondence" between the map and the environment. More recently, video recordings of people driving in cars have been analyzed to explore the sequential organiza-tion of talk and interaction between drivers and their passengers and of how people interrelate aspects of the visual environment and maps to find their way through an unknown neighborhood while driving (Brown and Laurier 2005; Laurier and Brown 2008; Mondada 2012).

People not only move through public spaces but also engage in a wide range of activities, both alone and with others. Goffman (1963) de-veloped conceptual distinctions to analyze the different displays of "in-volvement" in public. Drawing on this research, video-based studies of interaction in coffee shops and museums have furthered the knowledge of how people organize their activities in, and make sense of aspects of, the publicly visible or tangible environment (Laurier and Philo 2007). For example, Heath and vom Lehn, together with their colleagues at the Work Interaction and Technology Research Centre, have examined museum visitors' interaction and sense-making practices at the exhibit-face. Their studies reveal how people organize their talk and visual and bodily conduct to establish, if only momentarily, an alignment in their looking at and seeing works of art or other kinds of exhibit (Heath and vom Lehn 2004; Heath and vom Lehn 2012; vom Lehn, Heath, and Hindmarsh 2001; vom Lehn 2010b). They have also explored how visitors embed their use of technologies, such as interactive kiosks and mobile devices, in their interaction at exhibits and have illustrated how "interaction" with technologies often preoccupies people to the extent that they spend relatively little time looking at the original exhibit, and barely talk or interact in other ways with their companions (Heath and vom Lehn 2008; vom Lehn and Heath 2005a&b).

This body of research has been influential on recent debates in symbolic interactionism (Scott 2013), as well as in areas other than sociology, including education (see above), marketing, human-computer interaction, and computer-supported cooperative work. In marketing there has been a growing concern with experiential aspects of visiting shopping and retail settings, as well as museums and galleries (Schmitt 1999). Detailed studies of interaction in these domains, however, have rarely been conducted, as marketing and consumer research have largely relied on interview data and ethnographic observations. Video-based studies of interaction in museums complement this body of research by demonstrating the emergence of experience in interaction between people engaged in interaction with, and around, objects, artifacts, and technologies (vom Lehn 2006, 2010a). Related studies in shopping and retail environments have revealed the organization of queues at counters in retail banks and the organization of interaction between shop assistants and customers, including the sensitivity of shop assistants to customers' browsing behavior (Brown 2004; Brown and Laurier 2012; Clark, Drew, and Pinch 1994; Clark and Pinch 2009; Pinch and Clark 1986).

In addition to the contribution to the growing body of studies on behavior in public places, ethnomethodological research in these domains has informed research and practice in more applied fields, such as human-computer interaction (HCI) and computer-supported cooperative work (CSCW). Dourish's (2001; Dourish and Button 1998) theoretical and empirical analyses have helped to respecify common conceptions of action and collaboration that pervade debates in HCI and CSCW. Heath and Luff's (2000) studies have explicated how video-based studies of interaction in the control rooms of rapid urban transport systems can reveal how station staff observe and manage behavior in public places using complex assemblies of technology and people. Maybe surprisingly there has been considerable interest in HCI and CSCW in studies of museums and galleries, as these domains allow researchers to deploy and experiment with novel technologies and prototypes without endangering people's lives. This interest in the design implications of video-based studies has led to a number of "quasi-naturalistic experiments" in which researchers and designers have cooperated to develop and experiment with interactive artworks, as well as with craftwork designed to encourage interaction between people (Heath et al. 2002; Hindmarsh et al. 2002; Koleva et al. 2001; Patel et al. 2011).

This discussion of areas influenced by ethnomethodology is not exhaustive but only gives a brief glimpse into the pervasiveness of the program of research that originates in Garfinkel's writings on very many substantial debates in sociology. Curiously, the influence of ethnomethodology on sociology and its sub-areas is clearly visible, while ethnomethodology is often described as marginal and unimportant to sociology.

# Garfinkel's Orphans

On April 21, 2011 Paul ten Have, the system administrator of "ethno-Hotline," a digital distribution service for news of interest to ethno-methodologists, informed the subscribers of the listserv as well as his followers on Twitter that Harold Garfinkel had died:

> I've just been informed that Harold Garfinkel, founder, inventor and genius of ethnomethodology has passed away, so we are all 'orphans' now" (Paul ten Have, 21 April 2011, Twitter).

Paul ten Have's short note points to the immense importance that Garfinkel has had to the ethnomethodological community. He was the founder and point of reference for all those who see themselves as eth-nomethodologists. At the Conference of the International Institutes of Ethnomethodology and Conversation Analysis (IIEMCA) in Fribourg (Switzerland), tribute events were organized, where well-known eth-nomethodologists talked about their meetings and encounters with Garfinkel and his œvre (Endress and Psathas 2012). This was the tenth IIEMCA conference and is one of the important events where a sub-stantial number of ethnomethodologists meet on a regular basis.[1] Aside from this event, ethnomethodologists gather at the annual meetings of the American Sociological Society where they have their own sec-tion, Ethnomethodology and Conversation Analysis (EMCA), and ses-sions. Furthermore, there is the bi-annual International Conference on Conversation Analysis (ICCA) where, at the conference in Manheim in 2010, the International Society for Conversation Analysis (ISCA) was founded, which will further enhance the influence of conversation analysis in the future.[2]

This brief list of events and associations indicates that over the years, ethnomethodology and conversation analysis has become a very

*Harold Garfinkel: The Creation and Development of*
*Ethnomethodology* by Dirk vom Lehn. 167–170. © 2013 UVK
Verlagsgesellschaft mbH; additional material for English
edition © 2014 Left Coast Press, Inc. All rights reserved.

active community. Superficially seen, conversation analysis seems to have found a wider acceptance in the academic community, with large conferences and faculty positions in sociology and linguistics across the world. Yet it is ethnomethodology that is covered by sociological textbooks, with conversation analysis being discussed as one research strand based on Garfinkel's ethnomethodological program. Within these developments the relatively recent emergence of video-based studies of interaction has helped to invigorate an interest in ethnomethodology and conversation analysis both in academic debate and in commercial research laboratories. Furthermore, ethnomethodologists utilize their methodological liberalism and deploy ethnography, document analysis, and a range of other methods in their studies.

As the emergence of separate and distinct foundations such as IIEMCA and ISCA suggests, the institutionalization and development of ethnomethodology and conversation analysis has not happened without controversy. These arguments and debates within the field are not new but have been part of the history of ethnomethodology since the 1960s, as indicated by Psathas in a recent publication (Psathas 2008). Different "Schools" of ethnomethodology have arisen at universities in the USA as well as the UK, schools that are trying to differentiate their research from each other and, thereby, have not always agreed with each other's approaches (Flynn 2011). The importance of the discussions and debates within the field, however, have not hindered its development, rather they have helped to widen its scope and influence in other areas, such as the technical sciences.

Now, with Garfinkel's passing, ethnomethodology enters a new phase in its development. Their blossoming in the technical sciences most clearly indicates the impact ethnomethodological research can have beyond academia. In light of current public debate about the impact of the social sciences, ethnomethodologists now are at the forefront of a public sociology, i.e., a sociology that makes itself relevant outside the walls of academia and connects with stakeholders.

From the beginning of his empirical work at Howard Odum's Institute in Newark, Garfinkel saw sociology as inextricably intertwined with society, but at the same time as lacking a sociological attitude that allowed sociologists to describe society in an adequate way. In this book, I hope to have provided a glimpse into the development of this sociological attitude that now we know as ethnomethodology. Hopefully, in the coming years further so-far unpublished manuscripts from Garfinkel's archive, currently kept in Boston, will help us learn more about the origin and development of Garfinkel's program and continue to remind us that at the center of this program has always been the production of Durkheim's social facts.

# Notes

## Chapter 1

1. A pertinent example of the relationship between Garfinkel's early education in business and accounting and his later work is his paper "Good Reasons for Bad Clinical Records" (Garfinkel 1967h).

2. Later, conversational analysis was renamed and nowadays is known as conversation analysis.

3. Within this book I largely refer to Garfinkel's published work. I only mention in passing the unpublished manuscript *Parsons' Primer* (1960). His doctoral dissertation has not been published (yet) but it is accessible via microfiche.

4. In his critical review of Talcott Parsons' *Sociological Theory and Modern Society*, John Finley Scott (1968: 456, Fn 2) mentions Garfinkel's difficult style of writing which, in his view, has contributed to the cult status of ethnomethodology. To give his argument a particular flavor he also claims that students were reading Garfinkel's papers prior to their publication in private seminars with dimmed lights. Such characterizations of Garfinkel and ethnomethodology still pervade sociological books to the present day. For example, Martin (2011: xi) writes in his recent book that "Garfinkel instead put his own formulizations in between his students and the phenomenological tradition, acting more like a cult leader than a scholar."

5. His participation in seminars in Boston and Manchester supported the foundation of sociological faculties that offered training in ethnomethodology and conversation analysis (Flynn 2011; Psathas 2008).

6. Garfinkel drew his use of "praxeology" from Henry Hiz's (1954) paper "Kotarbinski's praxeology" (see Garfinkel 1956b).

## Chapter 2

1. In the years after its original publication in the magazine *Opportunity* in 1940, the short story was published two more times: first in a volume collecting the

best short stories of 1940 (Garfinkel 1941) and then in a collection of essays concerned with a critical exploration of interethnic relations (Garfinkel 1945).

2. Rawls (2013: 308) suggests that the piece is based on field observation of a racial incident, while Hama (2009) refers to it as a literary work. Hama's view resonates with Guy Johnson, Garfinkel's advisor in Chapel Hill, who described it as a "story" (Johnson 1941: 96). With reference to the preface of the story as published in *Opportunity*, Doubt (1989: 253) states that Garfinkel was an "eyewitness" to the event.

# Chapter 3

1. Rawls (2002) highlights the irony that a sociologist whose later works were to be concerned with the importance of practice had to rely on theoretical concepts of situations where people deal with life and death.

2. After the war, Parsons was particularly concerned with increasing the influence of his book (1937) *The Structure of Social Action* that, due to its publication close to the beginning of WW2, had not influenced sociology as much as he had hoped (Vidich 2000).

3. It may be interesting to add here that Parsons, who had been developing pattern variables since the 1950s, invited Garfinkel to work with him on a response to a critique of his theory by Robert Dubin (1960).

4. Later Parsons and Shils (1952) address this problem by introducing the concept of *double contingency*.

5. Garfinkel argued that Parsons' and Schutz's positions could be adapted to allow for the development of an approach that could be used to revise the phenomenological position that action and experience were unavoidably intertwined (Garfinkel 2006 [1948]). Parsons, however, did not see any advantage in taking onboard any of Schutz's suggestions. Further attempts by Schutz to persuade Parsons that both their approaches could be aligned in a worthwhile way remained without success. The two scholars ended their exchange by agreeing to disagree (Grathoff 1978).

6. Rawls (2002) presumes that Garfinkel delayed or even resisted the publication of this and other manuscripts because he increasingly felt that such theoretical and conceptual papers did not meet his own requirement of an "adequacy of description". While these descriptions can be read, they remain practically unintelligible to participants who are able to enact or embody them.

7. Pragmatism was developed in the nineteenth century by philosophers and social thinkers at the University of Chicago. They included William James, Charles Sanders Peirce, John Dewey and George Herbert Mead. Among other things,

pragmatism provides the theoretical basis for the development of symbolic inter-actionism as conceived by Mead's student, Herbert Blumer (1969).

8. Garfinkel described this knowledge and the practical competence of actors or "members" as *(ethno-) methods* (cf. 1967a).

9. Cicourel (1973) refers to the same phenomenon by describing actions as being oriented retrospectively and prospectively at the same time.

10. Garfinkel and other ethnomethodologists later described the sequential relation-ship between actions as *reflexive* (e.g., Lynch 2000a, Macbeth 2001).

11. Interactionists, for example, argue that the "definition of the situation" (Thomas 1967[1928]) is the basis for the emergence of social interaction.

12. In later works, Garfinkel and his students began to respecify further sociological concepts (Garfinkel 1967a; Lynch 1993).

13. More recently, Timothy Halkowski (1990) has used Garfinkel's respecification of *role* in a study of how participants use the concept of role to make sense of action and activities.

# Chapter 4

1. The "voluntaristic theory of action" is Parsons' (1937) contribution to debates about the context of action. Based on a detailed analysis of Alfred Marshall, Vilfredo Pareto, Emile Durkheim, and Max Weber's theoretical works, Parsons develops a theory that brings together ("convergence") the key arguments these classic sociologists had made about the relationship of action to the social world.

2. Garfinkel (2002: 72) later talked about deliberately "mis-reading" Schutz and other sociological classics (Eberle and Srubar 2010).

3. While in the trust paper Garfinkel used the term *basic rules*, he later referred to *methods* or *ethnomethods*. Thus, he removed himself from the analogy of the game when describing the organization of the everyday and tried to link his re-search program to other "ethno-sciences". His colleague, Aaron Cicourel (1973), replaced the term basic rules with "interpretive procedures".

4. "When I speak of accountable my interests are directed to such matters as the fol-lowing. I mean observable-and-reportable, i.e., available to members as situated practices of looking-and-telling" (Garfinkel 1967c: 1).

5. See the discussion of tic-tac-toe above.

6. When analyzing the experiments Garfinkel pointed out that he was indebted to Schutz's works. In a footnote to the paper "Studies of the Routine Grounds of Everyday Activities" he wrote: "Readers who are acquainted with his [Alfred Schutz] writings will recognize how heavily this paper is indebted to him" (Gar-finkel 1967d [1964]: 36, Fn. 1).

7. For a discussion of Garfinkel's "cultural dope" see Pleasants (1998) and Lynch (2012).
8. Sociology textbooks often describe Garfinkel's ethnomethodology as if its sole method of research were breaching experiments. While Garfinkel (2002) himself talked about "experiments" and "tutorial exercises", he never regarded them as "scientific experiments". Instead he deployed them as a means to learn about the social organization of the everyday (see Rawls 2002, 2008).

# Chapter 5

1. The presentation was published as "Some Rules of Correct Decision that Jurors respect" in Garfinkel's *Studies in Ethnomethodology* (1967f).

# Chapter 6

1. This argument is echoed by Watson (2009), who explores how Garfinkel develops a distinctive notion of trust as a background condition for mutually intelligible action.
2. Weber and Schutz, as well as Parsons' notion of historically comparable and generalizable propositions, are worthwhile remembering here.
3. The term *Weltanschauung* is difficult to translate. In the English version of Mannheim's chapter it remains untranslated; it denotes the framework of ideas and beliefs that guides people's perception and experience of the world
4. It is worthwhile noting that Garfinkel arranged for Gurwitsch's book to be translated.
5. Lynch (1993: 113) ascribes the idea of "the missing what" to Garfinkel.
6. Garfinkel already understood this relationship in his doctoral research. While his colleagues sat in the computer rooms at Harvard producing statistical representations of the social world, he was interested in the ways in which the data statistical analyses are based on, were gathered, coded and turned into accounts for social order.

# Chapter 7

1. Moore came to fame through his collaboration with Kingsley Davis and their studies of stratification (Davis and Moore 1945).
2. Garfinkel and colleagues (1981) derived the term *intertwining* from Merleau-Ponty (1995/1959).

# Chapter 8

1. Morana Alac (2011) has recently published an important laboratory study that explores the bodily, visual and material practices of scientists when examining fMRI brain scans. In her analysis, Alac combines the ethnomethodological attitude with Peirce's semiotics.

2. Lynch (2000c) and Lynch and Bogen (1996) examine the relationship between ethnomethodology and conversation analysis and are critical of the sometimes overly technical use of conversation analysis that ignores the fact that in its use of transcripts CA relies on a rhetorical device that operates just like the technical devices used by natural scientists to give their arguments a realist look (Bogen 1999).

# Chapter 9

1. The term "skid row" denotes a street that features cheap, often dilapidated pubs, bars, and hotels.

2. In his posthumous published lectures, Harvey Sacks (1992) refers to Simmel's paper (1970) on the importance of gaze exchanges for the organization of social situations. He suggests analyzing films of situations but, unfortunately, due to his premature death, did not conduct such studies himself.

# Postscript

1. The eleventh IIEMCA Conference was organized by Patrick Watson, Peter Eglin and Roy Turner at the Wilfrid Laurier University in Waterloo (Ontario, Canada) in 2013.

2. The next ICCA conference will be held at the University of Los Angeles in June 2014. It is expected to attract more than 600 attendees.

# References

Addams, Jane. 1912. "Recreation as a public function in urban communities." *American Journal of Sociology 17* (5): 615–619.

Alac, Morana. 2011. *Handling Digital Brains. A Laboratory Study of Multimodal Semiotic Interaction in the Age of Computers.* Cambridge, MA: MIT Press.

Antaki, Charles. 2011. *Applied Conversation Analysis: Intervention and Change in Institutional Talk.* Basingstoke: Palgrave Macmillan.

Appelrouth, Scott A., and Laura Desfor Edles. 2008. *Classical and Contemporary Sociological Theory: Text and Readings.* New York: Pine Forge Press.

Askins, Roy L., Timothy J. Carter, and Michael Wood. 1981. "Rule enforcement in a public setting: the case of basketball officiating." *Qualitative Sociology* 4 (2): 87–101.

Ayass, Ruth. 2007. *Kommunikation und Geschlecht.* Stuttgart: Kohlhammer.

Bales, Robert F. 1976 [1950]. *Interaction Process Analysis.* Chicago: University of Chicago Press.

Barber, Michael D. 2004. *The Participating Citizen: A Biography of Alfred Schutz.* New York: State University of New York Press.

Bateson, G., and J. Ruesch. 1951. *Communication: The Social Matrix of Psychiatry.* New York: Norton.

Bayley, David H., and Egon Bittner. 1984. "Learning the skills of policing." *Law and Contemporary Problems* 47 (4): 35–59.

Becker, Howard S. 1951. "The professional dance musician and his audience." *American Journal of Sociology.* 57 (2): 136–144.

Becker, Howard S., Blanche Geer, Everett C. Hughes, and Anselm S. Strauss. 1961. *Boys in White.* Chicago: University of Chicago Press.

Bell, Daniel. 1973. *The Coming of Post-Industrial Society.* New York: Basic Books.

Benson, Douglas, and John A. Hughes. 1983. *Perspective of Ethnomethodology.* Harlow: Longman.

Berard, Tim J. 2005. "Rethinking practices and structures." *Philosophy of the Social Sciences* 35 (2): 196–230.

_____. 2010. "Hate crimes and their criminalization." In *New Approaches to Social Problems Treatment,* edited by Mark Peyrot and Stacy Lee Burns, 15–40. Bingley: Emerald.

*Harold Garfinkel: The Creation and Development of*
*Ethnomethodology* by Dirk vom Lehn. 177–204. © 2013 UVK
Verlagsgesellschaft mbH; additional material for English
edition © 2014 Left Coast Press, Inc. All rights reserved.

_____. 2012. "Collective action, collective reaction: Inspecting bad apples in orga-nizational accounts for deviance and discrimination." In *Interaction and Every-day Life. Phenomenological and Ethnomethodological Essays in Honor of George Psathas*, edited by Hisashi Nasu and Frances Chaput Waksler, 261–278. Lanham, Maryland: Lexington Books.

Bergmann, Jörg. 1985. "Flüchtigkeit und methodische Fixierung sozialer Wirklichkeit: Aufzeichnungen als Daten der interpretativen Soziologie." In *Entzauberte Wissen-schaft: Zur Relativität und Geltung soziologischer Forschung*, edited by Wolfgang Bonß and Heinz Hartmann, 299–320. Goettingen: Schwarz.

Best, Katie. 2012. "Making museum tours better: Understanding what a guided tour really is and what a tour guide really does." *Museum Management and Curatorship* 27 (1): 35–52.

Bilmes, Jack. 1975. "Misinformation in verbal accounts: Some fundamental consider-ations." *Man* 10 (1): 60–71.

_____. 1993. "Ethnomethodology, culture, and implicature: Toward an empirical pragmatics." *Pragmatics* 3 (4): 387–409.

Bittner, Egon. 1961. *Popular Interests in Psychiatric Remedies: A Study in Social Control.* PhD Dissertation, University of California, Los Angeles.

_____. 1965. "The concept of organization." *Social Research* 32 (3): 239–258.

_____. 1967. "The police on skid-row: A study of peace keeping." *American Socio-logical Review* 32 (5): 699–715.

Bjelic, Dušan I. 1996. "Lebenswelt structures of Galilean physics: The case of Galileo's pendulum." *Human Studies* 19 (4): 409–432.

Bjelic, Dušan I. 2003. *Galileo's Pendulum.* New York: State University of New York Press.

Blum, Alan F. 1974. "Theorizing." In *Understanding Everyday Life*, edited by Jack D. Douglas, 301–319. London: Routledge & Kegan Paul.

Blum, Alan F, and Peter McHugh. 1971. "The social ascription of motives." *American Sociological Review* 36 (1): 98–109.

Blumer, Herbert. 1954. "What is wrong with social theory?" *American Sociological Re-view* 19 (1): 3–10.

_____. 1969. *Symbolic Interactionism: Perspective and Method.* New York: Prentice Hall.

Boden, Deidre. 1990a. "The world as it happens: Ethnomethodology and conversa-tion analysis." In *Frontiers of Social Theory: The New Synthesis*, edited by George Ritzer, 185–213. New York: Columbia University Press.

_____. 1990b. "People are talking: Symbolic interaction and conversation analysis", In *Symbolic Interaction and Cultural Studies*, edited by Howard S. Becker and Mi-chal M. McCall, 244–273. Chicago: University of Chicago Press.

_____. 1994. *The Business of Talk: Organizations in Action*. Cambridge: Polity Press.

Bogen, David. 1999. *Order Without Rules: Critical Theory and the Logic of Conversation*. New York: State University of New York Press.

Bogen, David, and Michael Lynch. 2007. "Do we need a general theory of social problems?" In *Reconsidering Social Constructionism: Debates in Social Problems Theory*, edited by James A. Holstein and Gale Miller, 213–239. New Brunswick, NJ: Transaction Publishers.

Bourdieu, Pierre. 1977. *Outline of a Theory of Practice*. Cambridge: Cambridge University Press.

Brazil, Wayne D. 1988. *Howard W. Odum: The Building Years, 1884–1930*. New York: Garland Publishers.

Broth, Matthias, and Frederik Lundstrom. 2013. "A walk on the pier. Establishing relevant places in a guided, introductory walk." In *Interaction and Mobility: Language and the Body in Motion*, edited by Pentti Haddington, Maurice Nevile, and Lorenza Mondada. Berlin: DeGryter.

Brown, Barry. 2004. "The order of service: The practical management of customer interaction." *Sociological Research Online* 9 (4).

Brown, Barry, and Eric Laurier. 2005. "Maps and car journeys: An ethno-methodological approach." *Cartographica* 4: 17–33.

_____. 2012. "Word of mouth: Product talk on the move." *Consumption, Markets and Culture*: 1–33.

Burke, Kenneth. 1992 [1945]. *A Grammar of Motives*. New York: Prentice Hall.

Burns, Stacy L. 1997. "Practicing law: A study of pedagogic interchange in a law school classroom." *Law in Action. Ethnomethodological and Conversation Analytic Approaches to Law*, edited by Max Traver, 265–288. Aldershot: Ashgate-Dartmouth.

_____. 2001. "'Think your blackest thoughts and darken them:' Judicial mediation of large money damage disputes." *Human Studies* 24(3): 227–249.

_____. 2005. *Ethnographies of Law and Social Control*. Amsterdam: Elsevier JAI Press.

Burns, Stacy L. and Mark Peyrot. 2008. "Reclaiming discretion judicial sanctioning strategy in court-supervised drug treatment." *Journal of Contemporary Ethnography*, 42(5): 720–744.

Busfield, Joan. 1968. "Review: *Studies in Ethnomethodology*." *British Journal of Sociology* 19 (3): 345.

Button, Graham. 1993. *Technology in Working Order: Studies of Work, Interaction, and Technology*. New York: Routledge.

Button, Graham, and Wes Sharrock. 2002. "Operating the production calculus: Ordering a production system in the print industry." *British Journal of Sociology* 53 (2): 275–289.

# References

_____. 2009. *Studies of Work and the Workplace in HCI: Concepts and Techniques.* San Rafael et al.: Morgan and Claypool Publishers.

Carlin, Andrew P., and Roger S. Slack. 2013. "Special Issue: Egon Bittner: Phenomenology in Action." *Ethnographic Studies* 13: 105–114.

Cicourel, Aaron V. 1973. "Interpretive procedures and normative rules in the negotiation of status and role." In *Cognitive Sociology: Language and Meaning in Social Interaction*, edited by ibid., 11–41, New York: The Free Press.

Cicourel, Aaron V., and John I. Kitsuse. 1963. *The Educational Decision Makers: An Advanced Study in Sociology.* Indianapolis, Indiana: Bobbs-Merril.

Clarke, John. 2001. "Social problems: Sociological perspectives." In *Understanding Social Problems: Issues in Social Policy*, edited by Margret May, Robert Page, and Edward Brunsdon, 3–15. Malden, MA: Wiley-Blackwell.

Clark, Colin, Paul Drew, and Trevor Pinch. 1994. "Managing customer 'objections' during real-life sales negotiations." *Discourse & Society* 5: 437–462.

Clark, Colin, and Trevor Pinch. 2009. "Some 'major' organisational consequences of some 'minor' organised behaviour: a Video analysis of pre-verbal service encounters in a showroom Retail store." In *Organisation, Interaction and Practice: Studies in Ethnomethodology and Conversation Analysis*, edited by Nick Llewellyn and Jon Hindmarsh, 140–171. Cambridge: Cambridge University Press.

Coleman, James S., Severyn T. Bruyn, and Anthony F. C. Wallace. 1968. "Review: *Studies in Ethnomethodology.*" *Social Forces* 33 (1): 126–130.

Coser, Lewis. 1975. "Two methods in search for a substance." *American Sociological Review* 400: 691–700.

Coulter, Jeff. 1983. *Rethinking Cognitive Theory.* London: Macmillan.

_____. 1989. *Mind in Action.* Cambridge: Polity Press.

_____. 2000. "Human practices and the observability of the macro-social." In *The Practice Turn in Contemporary Theory*, edited by Theodore R. Schatzki, Karin Knorr-Cetina, and Eike von Savigny, 29–41. London: Routledge.

_____. 2008. "Twenty-five theses against cognitivism." *Theory, Culture & Society* 25 (2): 19–32.

Coulter, Jeff, and Rod Watson. 2008. "The debate over cognitivism." *Theory, Culture & Society* 25 (2): 1–17.

Crabtree, Andy. 2001. *Wild Sociology.* unpublished PhD Thesis, University of Lancaster.

_____. 2003. *Designing Collaborative Systems: A Practical Guide to Ethnography.* Berlin: Springer.

Davis, Townsend. 1999. *Weary Feet, Rested Souls: A Guided History of the Civil Rights Movement.* New York: W. W. Norton & Co.

Davis, Kingsley, and Wilbert Moore. 1945. *Some Principles of Stratification.* Indianapolis, Indiana: Bobbs-Merril.

De Stefani, Elwys. 2010. "Reference as an interactively accomplished practice. Organizing spatial reorientation in guided tours." In *Spoken Communication Between Symbolics and Deixis*, edited by Massimo Pettorino et al., 137–170. Newcastle: Cambridge Scholars Publishing.

Denzin, Norman K. 1969. "Symbolic interactionism and ethnomethodology: A proposed synthesis." *American Sociological Review* 34 (6): 922–934.

Denzin, Norman K., and Yvonna S. Lincoln. 2011. *The SAGE Handbook of Qualitative Research*. London: Sage.

Dingwall, Robert. 2000. "Language, law, and power: Ethnomethodology, conversation analysis, and the politics of law and society studies (Book review)." *Law & Social Inquiry* 25 (3): 885–911.

Douglas, Jack D. 1974. *Understanding Everyday Life: Toward the Reconstruction of Sociological Knowledge*. London: Routledge & Kegan Paul.

Dupret, Baudouin. 2013. *Adjudication in Action*. Farnham: Ashgate.

Doubt, Keith. 1989. "Garfinkel before ethnomethodology." *The American Sociologist* 20 (3): 252–262.

Dourish, Paul. 2001. *Where The Action Is: The Foundations Of Embodied Interaction*. Cambridge, MA: MIT Press.

Dourish, Paul, and Graham Button. 1998. "On 'technomethodology': Foundational relationships between ethnomethodology and system design." *Human-Computer Interaction* 13 (4): 395–432.

Drew, Paul, and John Heritage. 1992. *Talk at Work: Interaction in Institutional Settings*. Cambridge: Cambridge University Press.

Dubin, Robert. 1960. "Parsons' actor: Continuities in social theory." *American Sociological Review* 25 (4): 457–466.

Durkheim, Emile. 1982 [1895]. *The Rules of Sociological Methods*. New York: The Free Press.

_____. 1997. [1893] *The Division of Labor*. New York: The Free Press.

Eberle, Thomas S. 1984. *Sinnkonstitution in Alltag und Wissenschaft. Der Beitrag der Phänomenologie an die Methodologie der Sozialwissenschaften*. Bern: Verlag Paul Haupt.

_____. 2008. "Phänomenologie und Ethnomethodologie." In *Phänomenologie und Soziologie*, edited by Jürgen Raab, Michaela Pfadenhauer, Peter Stegmaier, Jochen Dreher, and Bernt Schnettler, 151–161. Wiesbaden: Vs Verlag.

_____. 2012. "Phenomenology and sociology: Divergent interpretations of a complex relationship." In *Interaction and Everyday Life. Phenomenological and Ethnomethodological Essays in Honor of George Psathas*, edited by Hisashi Nasu and Frances Chaput Waksler, 135–152. Lanham: Lexington Books.

Eberle, Thomas S., and Ronald Hitzler. 2000. "Phänomenologische Lebensweltanaiyse." In *Qualitative Forschung. Ein Handbuch*, edited by Uwe Flick, 109–118. Reinbek: Rowohlt.

Eberle, Thomas S., and Ilja Srubar. 2010. "Einleitung." In *Zur Methodologie der Sozialwissenschaften*, edited by Alfred Schütz, Thomas S. Eberle, Jochen Dreher, and Gerd Sebald, 9–43. Konstanz: Universitaets Verlag Konstanz.

Eberle, Thomas S., and Christoph Maeder. 2011. "Organizational ethnography." In *Qualitative Research: Issues of Theory, Method and Practice*, edited by David Silverman, 53–74. Los Angeles: Sage.

Emirbayer, Mustafa, and Douglas W. Maynard. 2011. "Pragmatism and ethnomethodology." *Qualitative Sociology* 34 (1): 221–261.

Endress, Martin. 2009. "Two directions of continuing the Weberian project: Alfred Schutz and Talcott Parsons." In *Alfred Schutz and His Intellectual Partners*, edited by Hisashi Nasu, Lester Embree, George Psathas, and Ilja Srubar, 377–400. Konstanz: UVK Verlagsgesellschaft.

Endress, Martin, and George Psathas. 2012. "Introduction." *Human Studies* 35 (2): 149–151.

Engestrom, Yrjo, and David Middleton. 1998. *Cognition and Communication at Work*. Cambridge: Cambridge University Press.

Farber, Marvin. 2006. [1943]. *The Foundation of Phenomenology: Edmund Husserl and the Quest for a Rigorous Science of Philosophy*. New Jersey: Aldine Transaction.

Flynn, Pierce J. 2011. *The Ethnomethodological Movement. Sociosemiotic Interpretations*. Berlin: De Gryter Mouton.

Frankel, Richard M. 1984. "From sentence to sequence: Understanding the medical encounter through microinteractional analysis." *Discourse Processes* 7(2): 135–170.

Fulcher, James, and John Scott. 2007. *Sociology*. Oxford: Oxford University Press.

Gallant, Mary J., and Sherryl Kleinman. 1983. "Symbolic interactionism vs. ethnomethodology." *Symbolic Interaction* 6 (1): 1–18.

_____. 1985. "Making sense of interpretations: Response to Rawls on the debate between symbolic interactions and ethnomethodology." *Symbolic Interaction* 8 (1): 141–145.

Garfinkel, Harold. 1940. "Color trouble." In *Opportunity: A Journal of Negro Life*, (May).

_____. 1941. "Color trouble" in *The Best Short Stories of 1941 and the Yearbook of the American Short Story*, edited by E.J. O'Brien, 97–119, Boston: Houghton Mifflin.

_____. 1945. "Color trouble" in *Primer for White Folks*. edited by B. Moon, 269–286. New York: Doubleday.

_____. 1949. "Research note on inter- and intra-racial homicide." *Social Forces* 27, 369–381.

_____. 1952. *The Perception of the Other: a Study in Social Order*. Unpublished PhD Dissertation, Cambridge, MA: Harvard University

_____. 1956a. "Conditions of successful degradation ceremonies." *American Journal of Sociology* 61 (5): 420–424.

_____. 1956b. "Some sociological concepts and methods for psychologists." *Psychological Research Reports* 6: 181–195.

_____. 1960. *Parsons' Primer. Ad Hoc Uses.* Unpublished Manuscript, Los Angeles, California.

_____. 1963. "A conception of and experiments with 'trust' as a condition of stable concerted actions." In *Motivation and Social Interaction*, edited by O.J. Harvey, 187–238. New York: Ronald Press.

_____. 1967a. *Studies in Ethnomethodology.* Cambridge: Polity Press.

_____. 1967b. "Preface." In *Studies in Ethnomethodology*, vii–xi. Cambridge: Polity Press.

_____. 1967c. "What is ethnomethodology?" In *Studies in Ethnomethodology*, 1–34. Cambridge: Polity Press.

_____. 1967d. "Studies of the routine grounds of everyday activities." In *Studies in Ethnomethodology*, 35–75. Cambridge: Polity Press. (orig. in *Social Problems* 11 (3): 225–250, 1964.)

_____. 1967e. "Common-sense knowledge of social structures: The documentary method of interpretation in lay and professional fact finding." In *Studies in Ethnomethodology*, 76–103. Cambridge: Polity Press. (orig. in *Theories of the Mind*, edited by Jordan M. Scher, 1962. New York: Free Press, 689–712.)

_____. 1967f. "Some rules of correct decision making that jurors respect." In *Studies in Ethnomethodology*, 104–115. Cambridge: Polity Press.

_____. 1967g. "Passing and the managed achievement of sex status in an intersexed person, Part 1." In *Studies in Ethnomethodology*, 116–185. Cambridge: Polity Press.

_____. 1967h. "'Good organizational reasons for 'bad' clinical records.'" In *Studies in Ethnomethodology*, 186–207. Cambridge: Polity Press.

_____. 1967i. "Methodological adequacy in the quantitative study of selection criteria and selection practices in psychiatric outpatient clinics." In *Studies in Ethnomethodology*, 208–262. Cambridge: Polity Press.

_____. 1967j. "The rational properties of scientific and common sense activities." In *Studies in Ethnomethodology*, 262–283. Cambridge: Polity Press. (orig. in *Behavioral Science* 5 (1): 75–83.)

_____. 1967k. "Appendix to Chapter Five." In *Studies in Ethnomethodology*, 285–288. Cambridge: Polity Press.

_____. 1972. "Remarks on ethnomethodology." In *Directions in Sociolinguistics*, edited by John Gumperz and Dell Hymes, 301–324. New York: Holt, Rinehart and Winston.

_____. 1974. "The origins of the term 'ethnomethodology'." In *Ethnomethodology*, edited by Roy Turner, 15–18. Harmondsworth, UK: Penguin.

_____. 1986. *Ethnomethodological Studies of Work*. London: Routledge.

_____. 1988. "Evidence for locally produced, naturally accountable phenomena of order, logic, reason, meaning, method, etc. in and as of the essential quiddity of immortal ordinary society, (I of IV): An announcement of studies." *Sociological Theory* 6 (1): 103–109.

_____. 1991. "Respecification: Evidence for locally produced, naturally accountable phenomena of order,* logic, reason, meaning, method, etc. in and as of the essential haecceity of immortal ordinary society, (i)—an announcement of studies." In *Ethnomethodology and the Human Sciences,* edited by Graham Button, 10–19. Cambridge: Cambridge University Press.

_____. 1996. "Ethnomethodology's program." *Social Psychology Quarterly* 59 (1): 5–21.

_____. 1997. "Practical sociological reasoning: Some features in the work of the Los Angeles suicide prevention center." In *Law in Action. Ethnomethodological and Conversation Analytic Approaches to Law,* edited by Max Travers, 25–41. Aldershot: Ashgate.

_____. 2002. *Ethnomethodology's Program: Working Out Durkheim's Aphorism.* Boston, MD: Rowman & Littlefield Publishers.

_____. 2006. [1948]. *Seeing Sociologically: The Routine Grounds of Social Action.* Boulder, CO: Paradigm Publishers. (edited by Anne Rawls)

_____. 2007a. "Four relations between literatures of the social scientific movement and their specific ethnomethodological alternates." *In Orders of Ordinary Action,* edited by David Francis and Stephen Hester, 13–29. Aldershot: Ashgate.

_____. 2007b. "Lebenswelt origins of the sciences: Working out Durkheim's aphorism." *Human Studies* 30 (1): 9–56.

_____. 2008. *Toward a Sociological Theory of Information.* Boulder, CO: Paradigm Publishers. (edited by Anne Rawls)

_____. 2012. "The 'red' as an ideal object." *Ethnografia* 1: 19–31.

Garfinkel, Harold, and Kenneth Liberman. 2007. "Introduction: The Lebenswelt Origins of the Sciences." *Human Studies* 30 (1) (March): 9–56.

Garfinkel, Harold, and Eric Livingston. 2003. "Phenomenal field properties of order in formatted queues and their neglected standing in the current situation of inquiry." *Visual Studies* 18 (1): 21–28.

Garfinkel, Harold, Michael Lynch, and Eric Livingston. 1981. "The work of a discovering science construed with materials from the optically discovered pulsar." *Philosophy of the Social Sciences* 11 (2): 131–158.

Garfinkel, Harold, and Harvey Sacks. 1970. "On formal structures of practical action." In *Theoretical Sociology: Perspectives and Developments*, edited by J. C. McKinney and Edward A. Tiryakian, 337–366. New York: Appleton-Century-Crofts.

Garfinkel, Harold, and D. Lawrence Wieder. 1992. "Two incommensurable, asymmetrically alternate technologies of social analysis." In *Text in Context: Contributions to Ethnomethodology*, edited by Graham Watson and Robert M Seiler, 175–206. Newbury Park: Sage Publications.

Gellner, Ernest. 1975. "Ethnomethodology—re-enchantment industry or Californian way of subjectivity." *Philosophy of the Social Sciences* 5 (4): 431–450.

Giddens, Anthony. 1986. *The Constitution of Society: Outline of the Theory of Structuration*. Cambridge: Polity Press.

_____. 2009. *Sociology*. Cambridge: Polity Press.

Goffman, Erving. 1963. *Behavior in Public Places. Notes on the Social Organization of Gatherings*. New York: The Free Press.

_____. 1964. "The neglected situation." *American Anthropologist* 66 (6): 133–136.

_____. 1971. *Relations in Public. Microstudies of the Social Order*. New York: Basic Books.

_____. 1972. *Encounters. Two Studies in the Sociology of Interaction*. London: Penguin.

_____. 1983. "The interaction order: American Sociological Association, 1982 Presidential Address." *American Sociological Review* 48 (1): 1–17.

_____. 1990. [1959] *T.he Presentation of Self in Everyday Life*. London: Penguin.

Goldthorpe, John H. 1973. "Book review: A revolution in sociology?" *Sociology* 7 (3): 449–462.

Goodwin, Charles. 1981. *Conversational Organisation: Interaction Between Speakers and Hearers*. New York, London: Academic Press.

_____. 1997. "The Blackness of black: Color categories as situated practice." In *Discourse, Tools and Reasoning: Essays on Situated Cognition*, edited by Barbara Burge, Lauren B. Resnick, Roger Säljö, and Clotilke Pontecorvo, 111–140. Berlin, Heidelberg, New York: Springer.

_____. 2000. "Action and embodiment within situated human interaction." *Journal of Pragmatics* 32: 1489–1522.

_____. (ed.) 2002. *Conversation and Brain Damage*. New York: Oxford University Press.

_____. 2006. "Human sociality as mutual orientation in a rich interactive environment: Multimodal utterances and pointing in aphasia." In *Roots of Human Sociality*, edited by Nick Enfield and Stephen C. Levinson, 96–125. London: Berg.

Goodwin, Charles, and Marjorie H. Goodwin. 1996. "Seeing as situated activity: Formulating planes." In *Communication and Cognition at Work*, edited by Yirjo Engestrom and David Middleton, 61–95. Cambridge: Cambridge University Press.

Goodwin, Majorie H. 2006. *The Hidden Life of Girls: Games of Stance, Status, and Exclusion*. Chichester: Wiley-Blackwell.

Grathoff, Richard. 1978. *Theory of Social Action: Correspondence of Alfred Schutz and Talcott Parsons*. Bloomington: Indiana University Press.

Greiffenhagen, Christian. 2008. "Video analysis of mathematical practice? Different attempts to 'open up' mathematics for sociological investigation." *Forum Qualitative Sozialforschung / Forum: Qualitative Social Research* 9 (3). http://www.qualitative-research.net/index.php/fqs/article/view/1172/2585.

Greiffenhagen, Christian, and Wes Sharrock. 2008. "School mathematics and its everyday other? Revisiting Lave's 'Cognition in Practice." *Educational Studies in Mathematics* 69 (1): 1–21.

Gurwitsch, Aron. 2012. *The Collected Works of Aron Gurwitsch (1901–1973): Volume III: The Field of Consciousness: Theme, Thematic Field, and Margin*. New York: Springer.

Habermas, Jurgen. 1987. *Theory of Communicative Action. Lifeworld and System: A Critique of Functionalist Reason*. Boston: Beacon Press.

Hacket, Edward J., Olga Amsterdamska, Michael Lynch, and Judy Wajcman, (eds.). 2008. *The Handbook of Science and Technology Studies*. Cambridge, MA & London: The MIT Press.

Haddington, Pentti, Paul McIlvenny, and Mathias Broth. 2008. "Communicating place, space and mobility." *Journal of Pragmatics* 41 (10): 1879–2136.

Haddington, Pentti, Lorenza Mondada, and Maurice Nevile. 2013. *Interaction and Mobility: Language and the Body in Motion*. Berlin: deGruyter.

Halkowski, Timothy. 1990. "Role as interaction device." *Social Problems*, 37 (4): 564–577.

Hama, Hideo. 2009. "The primal scene of ethnomethodology: Garfinkel's short story 'Color Trouble' and the Schutz-Parsons controversy." In *Alfred Schutz and His Intellectual Partners*, edited by Hisashi Nasu, Lester Embree, George Psathas, and Ilja Srubar, 435–449. Konstanz: UVK Verlagsgesellschaft.

Hardesty, Monica J. 1982. "Ethnomethodology and symbolic interactionism: A critical comparison of temporal orientations." *Symbolic Interaction* 5 (1): 127–137.

Harper, Richard. 1997. *Inside the IMF: An Ethnography of Documents, Technology and Organisational Action*. London: Academic.

Hausendorf, Heiko. 2004. *Gespräch als System. Linguistische Aspekte einer Soziologie der Interaktion*. Radolfzell: Verlag fuer Gespraechsforschung.

Have, Paul ten. 2004. *Understanding Qualitative Research and Ethnomethodology*. London: Sage.

Heath, Christian. 1982. "The display of recipiency: An instance of a sequential relationship in speech and body movement." *Semiotica* 42 (2–4): 147–168.

_____. 1986. *Body Movement and Medical Interaction*. Cambridge: Cambridge University Press.

_____. 1989. "Pain talk: The expression of suffering in the medical consultation." *Social Psychology Quarterly* 52 (2): 113–125.

_____. 1992. "The delivery and reception of diagnosis in the general practice consultation." In *Talk at Work*, edited by Paul Drew and John Heritage, 165–189. Cambridge: Cambridge University Press.

_____. 2012. *The Dynamics of Auction: Social Interaction and the Sale of Fine Art and Antiques*. Cambridge: Cambridge University Press.

Heath, Christian, Hubert Knoblauch, and Paul Luff (2000). "Technology and social interaction: the emergence of 'workplace studies.'" *British Journal of Sociology* 51 (2): 299–320.

Heath, Christian, and Paul Luff. 2000. *Technology in Action*. Cambridge: Cambridge University Press.

Heath, Christian, Paul Luff, Dirk vom Lehn, Jon Hindmarsh, and Jason Cleverly. 2002. "Crafting participation: designing ecologies, configuring experience." *Visual Communication* 1 (1): 9–33.

Heath, Christian, and Dirk vom Lehn. 2004. "Configuring reception: (Dis-)regarding the 'spectator' in museums and galleries." *Theory, Culture & Society* 21 (6): 43–65.

_____. 2008. "Configuring 'interactivity': Enhancing engagement in science centres and museums." *Social Studies of Science* 38 (1): 63–91.

_____. 2012. "Revealing surprise: The local ecology and the transposition of action." In *Emotion in Interaction*, edited by Anssi Peräkylä and Marja-Leena Sorjonen, 215–234. Oxford and New York: Oxford University Press.

Helm, David T., (ed.) 1989. *The Interactional Order: New Directions in the Study of Social Order*. New York: Irvington Publishers.

Hemmings, Terry, David Randall, Lizz Marr, David Francis, and Stephen K. Hester. 2000. "Task, talk and closure: situated learning and the use of an 'interactive' museum artefact." In *Local Education Order Ethnomethodological Studies and Knowledge in Action*, edited by Stephen K. Hester and David Francis, 233–244. Amsterdam: John Benjamins.

Henderson, Kathryn, Jack Whalen, and Marilyn Whalen. 2002. "Improvisational choreography in teleservice work." *British Journal of Sociology* 53 (2): 239–258.

Heritage, John. 1984. *Garfinkel and Ethnomethodology*. Cambridge: Polity Press.

_____. 1988. "Explanations as accounts: A conversation analytic perspective." In *Analysing Everyday Explanation: A Casebook of Methods*, edited by Charles Antaki, 127–144. London: Sage.

_____. 2009. Conversation Analysis as Social Theory. In *The New Blackwell Companion to Social Theory*, edited by Bryan S. Turner, 300–320. Chichester: Wiley-Blackwell.

_____. 2010. "A Galilean moment in social theory? Language, culture and their emergent properties." *Qualitative Sociology* 34 (1): 263–270.

Heritage, John, and Tanya Stivers. 1999. "Online commentary in acute medical visits: A method of shaping patient expectations." *Social Science & Medicine* 49 (11): 16.

Heritage, John, and Douglas W. Maynard. 2006. *Communication in Medical Care: Interaction Between Primary Care Physicians and Patients*. Cambridge: Cambridge University Press.

Heritage, John, and Steven Clayman. 2010. *Talk in Action: Interactions, Identities, and Institutions*. Chichester: Wiley-Blackwell.

Hester, Stephen K., and David Francis. 2000. *Local Educational Order: Ethnomethodological Studies of Knowledge in Action*. Amsterdam: John Benjamins.

Hilbert, Richard A. 1992. *The Classical Roots of Ethnomethodology: Durkheim, Weber, and Garfinkel*. Chapel Hill: The University of North Carolina Press.

Hill, Richard J., and Kathleen Stones Crittenden. (eds.). 1968. *Proceedings of the Purdue Symposium on Ethnomethodology*. Purdue, IN: Institute for the Study of Social Change, Purdue University.

Hindmarsh, Jon. 2010. "Peripherality, participation and communities of practice: Examining the patient in dental training." In *Organisation, Interaction and Practice*, edited by Nick Llewellyn and Jon Hindmarsh, 218–240. Cambridge: Cambridge University Press.

Hindmarsh, Jon, and Christian Heath. 2000. "Embodied reference: A study of deixis in workplace interaction." *Journal of Pragmatics*. 32: 1855–1878.

Hindmarsh, Jon, Christian Heath, Dirk vom Lehn, and Jason Cleverly. 2002. "Creating assemblies: Aboard the ghost ship." In *Proceedings of the 2002 ACM Conference on Computer Supported Cooperative Work*. Chicago: ACM Publishers.

Hindmarsh, Jon, and Alison Pilnick. 2007. "Knowing bodies at work: Embodiment and ephemeral teamwork in anaesthesia", *Organization Studies*, 28(9): 1395–1416.

Hindmarsh, Jon, Patricia Reynolds, and Stephen Dunne. 2009. "Exhibiting understanding: The body in apprenticeship." *Journal of Pragmatics* 43 (2): 489–503.

Hirschauer, Stefan. 1998. "Performing sexes and genders in medical practice." In *Differences in Medicine: Unraveling Practices, Techniques, and Bodies*, edited by Marc Berg and Annemarie Bol, 13–27. Durham & London: Duke University Press.

Hiz, Henry. 1954. Kotarbinski's praxeology. *Philosophy and Phenomenological Research*. December: 451–463.

Holton, Gerald. 1981. "Comments on Professor Harold Garfinkel's paper." *Philosophy of the Social Sciences* 11 (2): 159–161.

Holstein, James A. and Gale Miller, (eds.). 1993. *Reconsidering Social Constructionism: Debates in Social Problems Theory*. Piscataway, NJ: Transaction Publishers.

Homans, George Caspar. 1961. *Social Behavior: Its Elementary Forms*. New York: Harcourt Brace.

_____. 1984. *Coming to My Senses: the Autobiography of a Sociologist.* New Brunswick, NJ: Transaction Books.

Hughes, Everett C. 1951. "Studying the nurse's work." *American Journal of Nursing* 51 (5): 294–295.

_____. 1984. *The Sociological Eye: Selected Papers.* New York: Transaction Publishers.

Hughes, John. 2001. "Of ethnography, ethnomethodology and workplace studies." *Ethnographic Studies* 6: 7–16.

Hughes, John, Val King, Tom Rodden, and Hans Andersen. 1994. "Moving out from the control room." In *Proceedings of the 1994 ACM Conference on Computer Supported Cooperative Work—CSCW,* 429–439. New York: ACM Press.

Husserl, Edmund. 2010. *Ideas: General Introduction to a Pure Phenomenonlogy.* Abingdon: Routledge.

Hutchinson, Phil, Rupert Read, and Wes Sharrock. 2008. *There Is No Such Thing as a Social Science: In Defence of Peter Winch.* Farnham: Ashgate Publishing Limited.

Ibarra, Peter R., and John I. Kitsuse. 1997. "An interactionist proposal for the study of social problems." In *Reconsidering Social Constructionism: Debates in Social Problems Theory,* edited by James A. Holstein and Gale Miller, 25–58. Piscataway, NJ: Transaction Publishers.

Jenkings, K. Neil. 2012. "Adjudicating accounts: A review of Dupret's ethnomethodological studies of Arab practices." *Symbolic Interaction* 36 (1): 99–103.

_____. 2009. "Garfinkel and his ethnomethodological 'bastards' Part 2", *Sociology* 43 (4): 775–781.

_____. 2006. "Garfinkel and his ethnomethodological 'bastards'", *Sociology* 40 (5): 957–963.

Joas, Hans. 1993. *Pragmatism and Social Theory.* Chicago: University Of Chicago Press.

Johnson, Guy B. 1941. "The Negro and crime." *Annals of the American Academy of Political and Social Science* 217: 93–104.

_____. 1955. "Howard Washington Odum: An appreciation." *Phylon* 16 (1): 101–102.

Johnson, Guy B., and Guion Griffis Johnson. 1980. *Research in Service to Society. The First Fifty Years of the Institute for Research in Social Science at the University of North Carolina.* Chapel Hill: The University of North Carolina Press.

Kalven, Harry, and Hans Zeisel. 1966. *The American Jury.* Boston: Little, Brown & Company.

Kaufmann, Felix. 1944. *Methodology of the Social Sciences.* London: Oxford University Press.

Kessler, Suzanne J., and Wendy McKenna. 1985. *Gender: An Ethnomethodological Approach.* Chicago: University of Chicago Press.

Kieserling, Andre. 1999. *Kommunikation unter Anwesenden. Studien ueber Interaktionssysteme.* Frankfurt am Main: Suhrkamp.

Kim, Kwan-ki., and Tim Berard. (2009). "Typification in society and social science: The continuing relevance of Schutz's social phenomenology." *Human Studies* 32 (3): 263–289.

Kitzinger, Celia. 2000. "Doing feminist conversation analysis." *Feminism & Psychology* 10 (2): 163–193.

Knoblauch, Hubert. 2000. "Review of André Kieserling, *Kommunikation unter Anwesenden. Studien ueber Interaktionssysteme.*" Frankfurt Am Main: Suhrkamp 1999. *Soziale Systeme* 6 (2): 389–392.

Knorr-Cetina, Karin, and Urs Bruegger. 2002. "Global microstructures: The virtual societies of financial markets." *American Journal of Sociology* 107 (4): 905–950.

Knorr-Cetina, Karin. 1981. *The Manufacture of Knowledge: An Essay on the Constructivist and Contextual Nature of Science.* Oxford: Pergamon.

Knorr-Cetina, Karin, and Michael Mulkay. 1983. *Science Observed. Perspectives of the Social Studies of Science.* London: Sage.

Knorr-Cetina, Karin, and Alex Preda. 2006. *The Sociology of Financial Markets.* Oxford: Oxford University Press.

Koleva, Boriana, Matt Adams, Ian Taylor, Steve Benford, Mike Fraser, Chris Greenhalgh, and Holger Schnädelbach. 2001. "Orchestrating a mixed reality performance." *Proceedings of the SIGCHI Conference on Human Factors in Computing Systems —CHI* (3): 38–45.

Koschmann, Timothy, Naomi Miyake, and Rogers P. Hall (eds.). 2002. *Rediscovering CSCL.* Hillsdale, NJ.: Lawrence Earlbaum Associates.

Koschmann, Timothy, Rogers P. Hall, and Naomi Miyake. 2002. *CSCL 2. Carrying Forward the Conversation.* Mahwah, NJ & London: Lawrence Earlbaum Associates.

Koschmann, Timothy. 2012a. "Early glimmers of the now familiar ethnomethodological themes in Garfinkel's 'The Perception of the Other.'" *Human Studies* 35 (4): 479–504.

_____. 2012b. "Team cognition and the accountabilities of the tool pass." In *Theories of Team Cognition: Cross-Disciplinary Perspectives,* edited by Eduardo Salas, Stephen Fiore, and Michael Letsky, 405–420, New York: Routledge.

Latour, Bruno. 1987. *Science in Action: How to Follow Scientists and Engineers through Society.* Cambridge, MA: Harvard University Press.

_____. 2005. *Reassembling the Social: An Introduction to Actor-Network-Theory.* Oxford: Oxford University Press.

Laurier, Eric. 2009. "Ethnomethodology/ethnomethodological geography." In *International Encyclopedia of Human Geography,* edited by Nigel Thrift and Robin Kitchen, 632–637. London: Elsevier Science.

Laurier, Eric, and Barry Brown. 2008. "Rotating maps and readers: Praxiological aspects of alignment and orientation." *Transactions of the Institute of British Geographers* 33: 201–221.

Laurier, Eric, and Chris Philo. 2007. "'A parcel of muddling muckworms': Revisiting Habermas and the English coffee-houses." *Social & Cultural Geography* 8 (2): 259–281.

Law, John. 1991. *A Sociology of Monsters: Essays on Power, Technology, and Domination.* London and New York: Routledge.

Lee, John R. E., and Rod Watson. 1993. *Plain Urbain. Interaction in Urban Public Space.* Unpublished Manuscript. Manchester.

Leiter, Kenneth. 1980. *A Primer on Ethnomethodology.* Oxford: Oxford University Press.

Liberman, Kenneth. 2013. *More Studies in Ethnomethodology.* New York: State University of New York Press.

Linton, Ralph. 1936. *The Study of Man.* New York: Appleton-Century-Crofts.

Liu, Yu Cheng. 2012. "Ethnomethodology reconsidered: The practical logic of social systems theory." *Current Sociology* 60 (5): 581–598.

Livingston, Eric. 1987. *Making Sense of Ethnomethodology.* Abingdon: Routledge.

Llewellyn, Nick. 2008. "Organization in actual episodes of work: Harvey Sacks and organization studies." *Organization Studies* 29 (5): 763–791.

Llewellyn, Nick, and Jon Hindmarsh (eds.). 2010. *Organisation, Interaction and Practice: Studies of Ethnomethodology and Conversation Analysis.* Cambridge: Cambridge University Press.

Luckmann, Thomas 1973. "Aspekte einer Theorie der Sozialkommunikation." In *Lexikon der germanistischen Linguistik*, edited by Hans Peter Althaus, Helmut Henne, and Herbert Ernst Wiegand, 1–13. Tübingen: Niemeyer.

Luff, Paul, Christian Heath, and Karola Pitsch. 2009. "Indefinite precision: The use of artefacts-in-interaction in design work." In *Routledge Handbook of Multimodal Analysis*, edited by Carey Jewitt, 213–224. London: Routledge.

Luff, Paul, Jon Hindmarsh, and Christian Heath. 2000. *Workplace Studies. Recovering Work Practice and Informing System Design.* Cambridge: Cambridge University Press.

Luhmann, Niklas. 1996. *Social Systems.* Edited by Dirk Baecker and John Bednarz. Stanford: Stanford University Press.

Lynch, Michael. 1985. *Art and Artefact in Laboratory Science: A Study of Shop Work and Shop Talk in a Laboratory.* Abingdon: Routledge.

_____. 1993. *Scientific Practice and Ordinary Action.* Cambridge: Cambridge University Press.

_____. 2000a. "Against reflexivity as an academic virtue and source of privileged knowledge." *Theory, Culture & Society* 17 (3): 26–54.

_____. 2000b. "Ethnomethodology and the logic of practice." In *The Practice Turn in Contemporary Theory*, edited by Theodore R. Schatzki and Karin Knorr-Cetina, 131–147. London: Routledge.

_____. 2000c. "The ethnomethodological foundations of conversation analysis." *Text—Interdisciplinary Journal for the Study of Discourse* 20 (4): 517–532.

_____. 2012. "Revisiting the Cultural Dope." *Human Studies* 35 (2): 223–233.

Lynch, Michael, Harold Garfinkel, and Eric Livingston. 1983. "Temporal order in laboratory work." In *Science Observed: Perspectives on the Social Study of Science*, edited by Karin Knorr-Cetina and Michael Mulkay, 205–238. London: Sage.

Lynch, Michael, and David Bogen. 1996. *The Spectacle of History: Speech, Text and Memory at the Iran-Contra Hearings*. Durham, NC: Duke University Press.

Macbeth, Douglas. 2001. "On 'reflexivity' in qualitative research: Two readings, and a third." *Qualitative Inquiry* 7: 35–68.

_____. 2003. "Hugh Mehan's learning lessons reconsidered: On the differences between the naturalistic and critical analysis of classroom discourse." *American Educational Research Journal* 40 (1): 239–280.

_____. 2012. "Some notes on the play of basketball in its circumstantial detail, and an introduction to their occasion." *Human Studies* 35 (2) (June 6): 193–208.

MacKenzie, Donald. 2005. "Opening the black boxes of global finance." *Review of International Political Economy* 12 (4): 555–576.

Mair, Michael, Chris Elsey, Patrick G. Watson, and Paul V. Smith. 2013. "Interpretive Asymmetry , Retrospective Inquiry and the Explication of Action in an Incident of Friendly Fire" *Symbolic Interaction* 36 (4): 398–416.

Mair, Michael, Patrick G. Watson, Chris Elsey, and Paul Vincent Smith. 2012. "War-Making and Sense-Making: Some Technical Reflections on an Instance of 'Friendly Fire." *The British Journal of Sociology* 63 (1): 75–96.

Mangione-Smith, Rita, Tanya Stivers, Marc Elliott, and Laurie McDonald. 2003. "Online commentary during the physical examination: A communication tool for avoiding inappropriate antibiotic prescribing?" *Social Science & Medicine* 56 (2): 313–320.

Mannheim, Karl. 1952. "On the interpretation of 'Weltanschauung'." In *From Karl Mannheim*, edited by Kurt H. Wolff, 33–83. New York: Oxford University Press.

Marlaire, Courtney L., and Douglas W. Maynard. 1990. "Standardized testing as an interactional phenomenon." *Sociology of Education* 63 (2): 83–101.

Marr, Liz, Gaby Porter, Dave Randall, Terry Hemmings, Dave Francis, and Colin Divall. 1997. "Situated knowledge and the virtual science and industry museum: Problems in the social-technical interface." *Archives and Museum Informatics* 11: 147–164.

Martin, John Levi. 2011. *The Explanation of Social Action*. New York: Oxford University Press.

Martin, David, John Mariani, and Mark Rouncefield. 2007. "Managing integration work in an NHS electronic patient record." *Health Informatics Journal* 13 (1): 47–56.

Maynard, Douglas W. 1988. "Language, interaction, and social problems" *Special Issue Social Problems* 35 (4): 311–334.

————. 1996. "Introduction of Harold Garfinkel for the Cooley-Mead Award." *Social Psychology Quarterly* 59 (1): 1–4.

Maynard, Douglas W., and Steven E. Clayman. 1991. "The diversity of ethnomethodology." *Annual Review of Sociology* 17: 385–418.

Maynard, Douglas W., and Courtney L. Marlaire. 1992. "Good Reasons for Bad Testing Performance: The Interactional Substrate of Educational Exams." *Qualitative Sociology* 15 (2): 177–202.

Maynard, Douglas W., and John Heritage. 2005. "Conversation analysis, doctor-patient interaction and medical communication." *Medical Education* 39 (4): 428–35.

McCabe, Rosemary, Christian Heath, Tom Burns, and Stefan Priebe. 2002. "Engagement of patients with psychosis in the consultation: Conversation analytic study." *British Medical Journal* 325: 1148–1151.

McDermott, Ray, Kenneth Gospodinoff, and Jeffrey Aron. 1978. "Criteria for an ethnographically adequate description of concerted activities and their contexts." *Semiotica* 24 (3/4): 245–276.

McHoul, Alexander W. 2008. "The organization of repair in classroom talk." *Language in Society* 19 (3): 349.

McHoul, Alexander W., and Mark Rapley. 2001. *How to Analyse Talk in Institutional Settings: A Casebook of Methods.* London: Continuum International.

Mead, George Herbert. 1926. "The objective reality of perspectives." In *Proceedings of the Sixth International Congress of Philosophy*, edited by Edgar S. Brightman, 75–85. New York.

————. 1932a. "The physical thing." In *The Philosophy of the Present*, 119–139. Chicago: University of Chicago Press.

————. 1932b. *The Philosophy of the Present.* Chicago: University of Chicago Press.

————. 1934. *Mind, Self, and Society from the Perspective of a Social Behaviorist.* Chicago: University of Chicago Press.

Mehan, Hugh. 1978. "Structuring school structure." *Harvard Educational Review* 48 (1): 32–65.

————. 1979. *Learning Lessons: Social Organization in the Classroom.* Cambridge, MA: Harvard University Press.

Mehan, Hugh, and Houston Wood. 1975. *The Reality of Ethnomethodology.* Chichester: John Wiley & Sons.

Meisner, Robin, Dirk vom Lehn, Christian Heath, Alex Burch, Ben Gammon, and Molly Reisman. 2007. "Exhibiting performance: Co-participation in science centres and museums." *International Journal of Science Education* 29 (12): 1531–1555.

Merleau-Ponty, Maurice. 1995 [1959]. *Phenomenology of Perception*. London and New York: Routledge.

Mills, C. Wright. 1940. "Situated actions and vocabularies of motive." *American Sociological Review* 5 (6): 904–913.

Mondada, Lorenza. 2003. "Working with video: How surgeons produce video records and their actions." *Visual Studies* 18 (1): 58–73.

_____. 2009. "Emergent focused interactions in public places: A systematic analysis of the multimodal achievement of a common interactional space." *Journal of Pragmatics* 41 (10) (October): 1977–1997.

_____. 2012. "Talking and driving: Multiactivity in the car." *Semiotica* 191: 223–256.

Mondada, Lorenza, and Simona Pekarek Doehler. 2004. "Second language acquisition as situated practice: Task accomplishment in the French second language classroom." *The Modern Language Journal* 88 (4): 501–518.

Moore, Robert J. 2012. "Ethnomethodology and Conversation Analysis: Empirical Approaches to the Study of Digital Technology in Action." In *Handbook of Digital Technology Research*, edited by Sara Price, Carey Jewitt, and Barry Brown, 217–235. New York & London: Sage.

Moore, Robert J., Jack Whalen, Hankinson Gathman, E. Cabell Gathman. (2010). "The work of the work order: Document practices in face-to-face service encounters." In N. Llewellyn & J. Hindmarsh (eds.), *Organisation, interaction and practice: Studies in Ethnomethodology and conversation analysis,* 172–197. Cambridge, UK: Cambridge University Press.

Münch, Richard. 1981. "Talcott Parsons and the Theory of Action I. The Structure of the Kantian Core." *American Journal of Sociology* 86 (4): 709-739.

_____. 1982. "Talcott Parsons and the Theory of Action II. The Continuity of the Development." *American Journal of Sociology* 87 (4): 771–826.

_____. 1993. *Sociological Theory: From the 1850s to the 1920s Vol 1*. Belmont, CA: Wadsworth Publishing Company.

O'Malley, Claire, Steve Benford, Andy Crabtree, Jonathan Green, Tony Pridmore, and Stuart Reeves. 2006. "The Spatial Character of Sensor Technology." In *Proceedings of DIS 2006*, 31–40. University Park, PA, USA: ACM.

Parry, Ruth H. 2006. Communication practices in physiotherapy: a conversation analytic study. In *Qualitative research for allied health professionals: challenging choices*, edited by Linda Finlay and Claire Ballinger (eds.), 108–124, New Jersey: John Wiley & Sons.

_____. 2013. "Giving reasons for doing something now or at some other time." *Research on Language and Social Interaction* 46 (2): 105–124.

Parsons, Talcott. 1937. *The Structure of Social Action (2 Volumes)*. New York: The Free Press.

————. 1951. *The Social System*. New York: The Free Press.

————. 1960. "Pattern variables revisited: A response to Robert Dubin." *American Sociological Review* 25 (4): 467–483.

Parsons, Talcott, and Edward A. Shils. 1952. *Toward a General Theory of Action*. Cambridge, Mass: Harvard University Press.

Patel, Menisha, Paul Luff, Christian Heath, Jason Cleverly, and Dirk vom Lehn. 2011. "Curious words and public definitions: Engaging visitors in the collaborative creation of a museum exhibit." In *Proceedings of Digital Engagement*. Newcastle, UK. http://de2011.computing.dundee.ac.uk/wp-content/uploads/2011/10/Curious-words-and-public-definitions-engaging-visitors-in-the-collaborative-creation-of-a-museum-exhibit.pdf

Peräkylä, Anssi, and Sanna Vehviläinen. 2003. "Conversation analysis and the professional stocks of interactional knowledge." *Discourse & Society* 14 (6): 727–750.

Peräkylä, Anssi, Charles Antaki, Sanna Vehviläinen, and Ivan Leudar. 2008. *Conversation Analysis and Psychotherapy: Psychotherapy in Practice*. Cambridge: Cambridge University Press.

Peyrot, Mark. 1982. "Understanding ethnomethodology: A remedy for some common misconceptions." *Human Studies* 5 (1): 261–283.

Peyrot, Mark, and Stacy L. Burns. 2001. "Sociologists on trial: Theoretical competition and juror reasoning." *The American Sociologist*. 32 (4): 42–69.

Pilnick, Alison. 2004. 'It's just one of the best tests we've got at the moment': The presentation of nuchal translucency screening for fetal abnormality in pregnancy, *Discourse and Society,* 15 (4): 451–465.

Pilnick, Alison and Olga Zayts. 2012. "'Let's have it tested first': Choice and circumstances in decision-making following positive antenatal screening in Hong Kong", *Sociology of Health and Illness*. 34(2): 266–282.

Pinch, Trevor, and Colin Clark. 1986. "The hard sell: `Patter merchanting' and the strategic (re)production and local management of economic reasoning in the sales routines of market pitchers." *Sociology* 20 (2): 169–191.

Pleasant, Nigel. 1998. "Experimentation in the social sciences: Cultural dope or reflexive agent? A reflexive critique of ethnomethodology." *Ethnographic Studies* 3 (3): 17–40.

Popper, Karl. 2002 [1934]. *The Logic of Scientific Discovery*. Abingdon: Routledge.

Psathas, George. 1986. "Some sequential structures in direction-giving." *Human Studies* 9 (2–3): 231–246.

————. 1999. "On the study of human action: Schutz and Garfinkel on social science." In *Schutzian Social Science*, edited by Lester Embree, 47–68. New York: Springer.

_____. 2004. "Alfred Schutz's influence on American sociologists and sociology." *Human Studies* 27 (1): 1–35.

_____. 2008. "Reflections on the history of ethnomethodology: The Boston and Manchester 'Schools'." *The American Sociologist* 39 (1): 38–67.

_____. 2009. "The correspondence of Alfred Schutz and Harold Garfinkel: What was the 'terra incognita' and the 'treasure island?'" In *Alfred Schutz and His Intellectual Partners*, edited by Hisashi Nasu, Lester Embree, Ilja Srubar, and George Psathas, 401–433, Konstanz: UVK Verlagsgesellschaft.

Raab, Jürgen. 2008. *Erving Goffman*. Konstanz: UVK Verlagsgesellschaft.

Randall, Dave, Richard Harper, and Mark Rouncefield. 2000. *Organisational Change and Retail Finance*. London & New York: Routledge.

Randall, Dave, Liz Marr, and Mark Rouncefield. 2001. "Ethnography, ethnomethodology and interaction analysis." *Ethnographic Studies* 6: 31–44.

Randall, Dave, Dan Shapiro, and John A. Hughes. 1992. "Faltering from ethnography to design." In *Proceedings of CSCW '92 Proceedings of the 1992 ACM conference on Computer-supported cooperative work*, 115–122. New York: ACM.

Rawls, Anne W. 1985. "Reply to Gallant and Kleinman on symbolic interactionism vs. ethnomethodology." *Symbolic Interaction* 8(1): 121–140.

_____. 1987. "The interaction order sui generis: Goffman's contribution to social theory." *Sociological Theory* 5: 136–149.

_____. 1989a. "Interaction Order or interaction ritual: Comment on Collins." *Symbolic Interaction* 12 (1): 103–109.

_____. 1989b. "An ethnomethodological perspective on social theory." In *The Interactional Order. New Directions in the Study of Social Order*, edited by David T. Helm, W. Timothy Anderson, Albert Jay Neehand, and Anne Warfield Rawls, 4–20. New York: Irvington Publishers.

_____. 2002. "Editor's introduction." In Harold Garfinkel, *Ethnomethodology's Program: Working Out Durkheim's Aphorism*, edited by Anne Warfield Rawls, 1–100. Lanham: Rowman and Littlefield.

_____. 2003a. "Harold Garfinkel." In *Harold Garfinkel*, edited by Michael Lynch and Wes Sharrock, 9–42. London: Sage.

_____. 2003b. "Orders of interaction and intelligibility: Intersections between Goffman and Garfinkel by way of Durkheim." In *Goffman's Legacy*, edited by A. Javier Trevino, 216–252. Lanham: Rowman and Littlefield.

_____. 2006. "Respecifying the study of social order—Garfinkel's transition from theoretical conceptualization to practices in details." In Harold Garfinkel, *Seeing Sociologically*, 1–97. Boulder, Colorado: Paradigm Publishers.

_____. 2007. "Harold Garfinkel." In *The Blackwell Companion to Major Contemporary Social Theorists*, edited by Michael Lynch and Wes Sharrock, 9–42. Oxford: Blackwell.

_____. 2008a. "Harold Garfinkel, ethnomethodology and workplace studies." *Organization Studies* 29 (5) (May 1): 701–732.

_____. 2008b. "Editor's introduction." In *Toward a Sociological Theory of Information*, edited by Anne Warfield Rawls, 9:1–100. Boulder, Colorado: Paradigm Publishers.

_____. 2009. *Epistemology and Practice: Durkheim's The Elementary Forms of Religious Life*. Cambridge: Cambridge University Press.

_____. 2013. "The early years, 1939–1953: Garfinkel at North Carolina, Harvard and Princeton." *Journal of Classical Sociology* 13 (2) (May 22): 303–312.

Rogers, Mary F. 1983. S*ociology, Ethnomethodology, and Experience. A Phenomenological Critique*. Cambridge: Cambridge University Press.

Rooke, John Alfred, and Mike Kagioglou. 2007. "Criteria for evaluating research: The unique adequacy requirement of methods". *Construction Management and Economics* 25 (9): 979–987.

Rouncefield, Mark, and Peter Tolmie. 2011. *Ethnomethodology at Work*. Farnham: Ashgate.

Ryave, A. Lincoln, and James N. Schenkein. 1974. "Notes on the art of walking." In *Ethnomethodology: Selected Readings*, edited by Roy Turner, 265–274. Middlesex: Penguin.

Sacks, Harvey. 1963. "Sociological description". *Berkeley Journal of Sociology* 8: 1–16.

_____. 1966. *The Search for Help: No One to Turn To*. Unpublished PhD Dissertation. Berkeley, CA: University of California at Berkeley.

_____. 1972. "Notes on police assessment of moral character." In *Studies in Social Interaction*, edited by David Sudnow, 280–293. New York: The Free Press.

_____. 1992. *Lectures on Conversation*. Victoria. Vol. I. Oxford: Blackwell Publishing.

Sacks, Harvey, Emanuel A. Schegloff, and Gail Jefferson. 1974. "A simplest systematics for the organization of turn-taking for conversation." *Language*. 50: 696–735.

Samra-Fredericks, Dalvir. 2004. "Managerial elites making rhetorical and linguistic 'moves' for a moving (emotional) display." *Human Relations* 57 (9): 1103–1143.

Samra-Fredericks, Dalvir, and F. Bargiela-Chiappini. 2008. "Introduction to the symposium on The Foundations of Organizing: The contribution from Garfinkel, Goffman and Sacks." *Organization Studies* 29 (5): 653–675.

Sarangi, Srikant, and Celia Roberts. 1999. *Talk, Work and Institutional Order: Discourse in Medical, Mediation and Management Settings*. Berlin: Mouton de Gruyter.

Schatzki, Theodore R., Karin Knorr-Cetina, and Eike von Savigny. 2000. *The Practice Turn in Contemporary Theory*. London & New York: Routledge.

Scheflen, Albert E. 1973. *Communicational Structure*. Bloomington: Indiana University Press.

_____. 1974. *How Behavior Means*. New York: Gordon and Breach.

Schegloff, Emanuel A. 1989. "Harvey Sacks—Lectures 1964–1965 an introduction/ memoir." *Human Studies* 12 (3): 185–209.

_____. 1992. "Introduction." In *Lectures on Conversation*, edited by Harvey Sacks, 1: ix–lxiv. Oxford: Blackwell.

_____. 1999. "On Sacks on Weber on ancient Judaism: Introductory notes and interpretive resources." *Theory, Culture & Society* 16 (1): 1–29.

_____. 2007a. *Sequence Organization in Interaction. A Primer in Conversation Analysis*. Volume 1. Cambridge: Cambridge University Press.

_____. 2007b. "A tutorial on membership categorization." *Journal of Pragmatics* 39 (3): 462–482.

Schelting, Alexander von. 1934. *Max Webers Wissenschaftslehre*. Tübingen: J.C.B. Mohr.

Schmitt, Bernd. 1999. "Experiential marketing." *Journal of Marketing Management* 15 (1–3): 53–67.

Schneider, Wolfgang Ludwig. 2000. "The sequential production of social acts in conversation." *Human Studies* 23 (2): 123–144.

Schutz, Alfred. 1943. "The problem of rationality in the world." *Economica* 10 (38): 130–149.

_____. 1945a. "Some leading concepts of phenomenology." *Social Research* 12 (1): 77–97.

_____. 1945b. "On multiple realities." *Philosophy and Phenomenological Research* 5 (4): 533–576.

_____. 1953. "Common-sense and scientific interpretation of human action." *Philosophy and Phenomenological Research* 14 (1): 1–38.

_____. 1967a. *Collected Papers I. The Problem of Social Reality*. The Hague: Martinus Nijhoff.

_____. 1967b [1932]. *Phenomenology of the Social World*. Evanston, IL: Northwestern University Press.

_____. 1970. *Reflections on the Problem of Relevance*. Yale University Press.

Schutz, Alfred, and Thomas Luckmann. 1974. *Structures of the Life-World*. Amsterdam: Heinemann.

Scott, Susie, Tamsin Hinton-Smith, Vuokko Härmä, and Karl Broome. 2013. "Goffman in the Gallery: Interactive Art and Visitor Shyness." *Symbolic Interaction* 36 (4): 417–438.

Scott, John Finlay. 1968. "Review: Talcott Parsons' 'Sociological Theory and Modern Society.' *American Sociological Review* 33 (3): 453–456.

Shannon, Claude E., and Warren Weaver. 1949. *The Mathematical Theory of Information*. Urbana: University of Illinois Press.

Sharrock, Wes, and D. Rod Watson. 1984. "What's the point of 'rescuing motives'?" *The British Journal of Sociology* 35 (3): 435–449.

Sharrock, Wes, and Jeff Coulter. 1998. "On what we can see." *Theory & Psychology* 8 (2): 147–164.

Silbey, Susan S., and Egon Bittner. 1982. "The availability of law." *Ethnographic Studies* 13: 217–246.

Silverman, David. 1970. *Theory of Organisations*. Amsterdam & London: Heinemann.

————. 1998. *Harvey Sacks: Social Science and Conversation Analysis*. Oxford: Oxford University Press.

Simmel, Georg. 1970. "The Natural Forms of Communication. Sociology of the Senses: Visual Interaction." In *Introduction to the Science of Sociology*, edited by Ernest W. Burgess and Robert E. Park, 356–361. Chicago and London: The University of Chicago Press.

Simpson, Barbara. 2009. "Pragmatism, Mead and the practice turn." *Organization Studies* 30 (12): 1329–1347.

Smith, Greg. 2006. *Erving Goffman*. Oxford: Routledge.

Sormani, Philippe. 2011. "The Jubilatory YES! On the instant appraisal of an experimental finding." *Ethnographic Studies* 12: 59–77.

Sormani, Philippe, Esther González-Martínez, and Alain Esther Bovet, 2011. "Special issue: Discovering work: Ethnomethodological studies in the natural sciences." http://www.zhbluzern.ch/index.php?id=2584. *Ethnographic Studies* 12.

Speer, Susan A., and Elizabeth H. Stokoe. 2011. *Conversation and Gender*. Cambridge: Cambridge University Press.

Spiegelberg, Herbert. 1981 [1960]. *The Phenomenological Movement: A Historical Introduction*. New York: Springer.

Stevens, Mitchell L., and Wendy Nelson Espeland. 2005. "Commensuration." *Encyclopedia of Social Measurement*. Academic Press: 375–378.

Stivers, T. 2005. "Non-antibiotic treatment recommendations: Delivery formats and implications for parent resistance." *Social Science & Medicine* 60(5): 949–964.

Stivers, T. 2006. "Treatment decisions: Negotiations between doctors and parents in acute care encounters." In *Communication in Medical Care: Interaction Between Primary Care Physicians and Patients*, edited by John Heritage and Douglas W. Maynard, 279–311. Cambridge: Cambridge University Press.

Stokoe, Elizabeth H. 2000. "Toward a conversation analytic approach to gender and discourse." *Feminism & Psychology* 10 (4): 552–563.

————. 2003. "Doing gender, doing categorization: Recent developments in language and gender research." *International Sociolinguistics* 2 (1): 1–12.

————. 2006. "On Ethnomethodology, feminism, and the analysis of categorical reference to gender in talk-in-interaction." *The Sociological Review* 54 (3): 467–494.

_____. 2010. "'I'm not gonna hit a lady': Conversation analysis, membership categorization and men's denials of violence towards women." *Discourse & Society* 21 (1): 59–82.

Suchman, Lucy. 1996. "Constituting shared workspaces." In *Cognition and Communication at Work*, edited by David Middleton and Yirjo Engestrom. Cambridge: Cambridge University Press.

_____. 2006. *Human and Machine Reconfigurations: Plans and Situated Actions*. Cambridge: Cambridge University Press.

Sudnow, David. 1967. *Passing On. The Social Organization of Dying*. Upper Saddle River, NJ: Prentice Hall.

_____. 1979. *Ways of the Hand. The Organization of Improvised Conduct*. New York: Bantam.

_____. 2000. *Pilgrim in the Microworld*. New York: Warner Books.

Svensson, Marcus Sanchez, Paul Luff, and Christian Heath. 2009. "Embedding instruction in practice: Contingency and collaboration during surgical training." *Sociology of Health & Illness*, 31 (6): 889–906.

Swanson, Guy, Anthony Wallace, and James Coleman. 1968. "Review symposium of Harold Garfinkel's *Studies in Ethnomethodology*." *American Sociological Review* 33: 122–124.

Szymanski, Margret, and Jack Whalen. 2011. *Making Work Visible: Ethnographically Grounded Case Studies of Work Practice*. Cambridge: Cambridge University Press.

Thielmann, Tristan. 2012. "Taking into account." *Zeitschrift für Medienforschung* 6 (1): 72–89.

Thomas, William I. 1967 [1928]. "The definition of the situation." In *Symbolic Interaction: Reader in Social Psychology*, edited by Bernard N. Meltzer and Jerome G. Manis, 315–321. Boston: Allyn & Bacon.

Thomas, William I., and Florian Znaniecki. 1920. *The Polish Peasant in Europe and America*. Chicago: University of Chicago Press.

Toffler, Alvin. 1981. *The Third Wave*. New York: Pan Books.

Travers, Max. 1997. *The Reality of Law: Work and Talk in a Firm of Criminal Lawyers*. Aldershot: Ashgate.

Travers, Max, and John F. Manzo. 1997. *Law in Action: Ethnomethodological and Conversation Analytic Approaches to Law*. Farnham: Ashgate.

Turner, Roy. 1974. *Ethnomethodology: Selected Readings*. London: Penguin.

Vidich, Arthur J. 2000. "The Department of Social Relations and systems theory at Harvard: 1948–50." *International Journal of Politics, Culture and Society* 13 (4): 607–648.

Vinkhuyzen, Erik, and Jack Whalen. 2000. "Expert systems in (inter)action: Diagnosing document machine problems over the telephone." In *Workplace Studies*, edited by Paul Luff, Jon Hindmarsh, and Christian Heath, 92–140. Cambridge: Cambridge University Press.

Vinkhuyzen, Erik, Alison Woodruff, Margaret H. Szymanski, and Paul M. Aoki. 2006. "Organizing a remote state of incipient talk: Push-to-talk mobile radio interaction." *Language in Society* 35 (3): 393–418.

vom Lehn, D. 2013. "Withdrawing from exhibits: The Interactional organisation of museum visits." In *Interaction and Mobility: Language and the Body in Motion*, edited by Pentti Haddington, Lorenza Mondada, and Maurice Nevile, 65–90. Berlin: deGryter.

_____. 2012. "Configuring standpoints: Aligning perspectives in art exhibitions." *Bulletin Suisse de Linguistique Appliquée* 96: 69–90.

_____. 2010a. "Examining 'response': Video-based studies in museums and galleries." *International Journal of Culture, Tourism and Hospitality Research* 4 (1): 33–43.

_____. 2010b. "Discovering 'experience-ables': Socially including visually impaired people in art museums." *Journal of Marketing Management* 26 (7–8): 749–769.

_____. 2006. "Embodying Experience: A Video-Based Examination of Visitors' Conduct and Interaction in Museums." *European Journal of Marketing* 40 (11/12): 1340–1359.

vom Lehn, D., Helena Webb, Will Gibson, and Christian Heath. 2012. "Assessing distance vision as interactional achievement: A study of commensuration in action." *Soziale Welt* 64 (1–2): 115–136.

vom Lehn, D., and Christian Heath. 2005a. "Rethinking interactivity: Design for participation in museums and galleries." In *Rethinking Interactivity*, edited by Liam Bannon, Luigina Ciolfi, and Tony Hall. Limerick: University of Limerick. http://www.academia.edu/193814/Rethinking_Interactivity

_____. 2005b. "Accounting for new technology in museum exhibitions." *International Journal of Arts Management* 7 (6): 11–21.

vom Lehn, D., Christian Heath, and Jon Hindmarsh. 2001. "Exhibiting interaction: Conduct and collaboration in museums and galleries." *Symbolic Interaction* 24 (2): 189–216.

Vygotsky, Lev S., and Michael Cole. 1978. *Mind in Society: The Development of Higher Psychological Processes*. Cambridge, Mass. & London: Harvard University Press.

Wagner, Helmut R. 1986. *Alfred Schutz: An Intellectual Biography*. Chicago: University of Chicago Press.

Watson, Rod. 2009. "Constitutive practices and Garfinkel's notion of trust: Revisited." *Journal of Classical Sociology* 9 (4): 475–499.

Webb, Helena. 2009. "'I've put weight on cos I've bin inactive, cos I've 'ad me knee done': Moral work in the obesity clinic." *Sociology of Health & Illness* 31 (6): 854–71.

Webb, Helena, Christian Heath, Dirk vom Lehn, and William Gibson. 2013. "Engendering Response: Professional Gesture and the Assessment of Eyesight in Optometry Consultations." *Symbolic Interaction* 36 (2): 137–158.

References

Weber, Max. 1998 [1948]. *From Max Weber: Essays in Sociology*, edited by Hans Heinrich Gerth and C. Wright Mills. Abingdon: Routledge.

————. 2010. [1949]. *Methodology of Social Sciences*. Edited by Edward Shils and Henry A. Finch. New Jersey: Transaction Publishers.

Wertsch, James. 1991. *Voices of the Mind*. London: Harvester Wheatsheaf.

West, Candace, and Don H. Zimmerman. 1987. "Doing gender." *Gender & Society* 1 (2): 125–151.

————. 2009. "Accounting for doing gender." *Gender & Society* 12: 112–123.

Whalen, Jack, and Don H. Zimmerman. 2005. "Working a call: Multiparty management and interactional infrastructure in calls for help." In *Calling for Help: Language and Social Interaction in Telephone Helplines*, edited by Michael Emmison, Alan Firth, and Carolyn D. Baker, 309–345. Amsterdam: John Benjamins.

Whalen, Marilyn R., Jack Whalen, Robert J. Moore, Geoffrey Raymond, Margaret H. Szymanski, and Erik Vinkhuyzen. 2004. "Studying workscapes." In *Discourse and Technology: Multimodal Discourse Analysis*, edited by Philip LeVine and Ron Scollon, 208–229. Washington, DC: Georgetown University Press.

Wieder, D. Lawrence. 1974. *Language and Social Reality: The Case of Telling the Convict Code*. The Hague: Mouton.

Wilkins, James. 1968. "Review: Studies in ethnomethodology." *American Journal of Sociology* 73 (5): 642–643.

Wilson, Thomas P, and Don H. Zimmerman. 1979. "Ethnomethodology, sociology and theory." *Humboldt Journal of Social Relations* 7 (1): 52–88.

Wittgenstein, Ludwig. 1973 [1951]. *Philosophical Investigations*. Edited by G.E. Margaret Anscombe. London: Pearson.

Woolgar, Steve, and Michael Lynch. 1990. *Representation in Scientific Practice*. Cambridge, MA: MIT Press.

Wootton, Anthony J. 2005. *Interaction and the Development of Mind*. Cambridge: Cambridge University Press.

————. 2006. "Children's practices and their connections with 'mind.'" *Discourse Studies* 8 (1): 191–198.

Zimmerman, Don H., and Melvin Pollner. 1970. "The everyday world as phenomenon." In *Understanding Everyday Life*, edited by Jack D. Douglas, 33–65. Chicago: Aldine.

Zimmerman, Don H., Lawrence D. Wieder, and Siu Zimmerman. 1976. *Understanding Social Problems*. New York: Praeger.

Znaniecki, Florian. 1936. *Social Actions*. New York: Farrar & Rinehart.

# Subject Index

# Name Index

# About the Author

Dirk vom Lehn is a member of the Work, Interaction and Technology Research Centre in the Department of Management at King's College London. His research is primarily concerned with video-based studies of interaction in museums and galleries as well as in optometric practices. He is currently one of the co-chairs of the Section "Ethnomethodology and Conversation Analysis" at the American Sociological Association, and book review editor of *Symbolic Interaction*.

39092 08976375 1